THE ALLOCATION OF HEALTH CARE RESOURCES

Titles in the Series:

Medico-Legal Aspects of Reproduction and Parenthood, Second Edition
J.K. Mason, University of Edinburgh

Intersections: Women on Law, Medicine and Technology
Edited by *Kerry Petersen,* La Trobe University

Law Reform and Human Reproduction
Edited by *Sheila A.M. McLean,* University of Glasgow

Legal Issues in Human Reproduction
Edited by *Sheila A.M. McLean,* University of Glasgow

Mental Illness: Prejudice, Discrimination and the Law
Tom Campbell, Australian National University, Canberra and
Chris Heginbotham, Riverside Mental Health Trust, London

Pregnancy at Work
Noreen Burrows, University of Glasgow

Changing People: The Law and Ethics of Behaviour Modification
Alexander McCall Smith, University of Edinburgh

Health Resources and the Law: Who Gets What and Why
Robert G. Lee, Cardiff Law School and *Frances H. Miller,* University of Boston

Surrogacy and the Moral Economy
Derek Morgan, Cardiff Law School

Family Planning Practice and the Law
Kenneth McK. Norrie, University of Strathclyde

Mental Health Law in Context: Doctors' Orders?
Michael Cavadino, University of Sheffield

Artificial Reproduction and Reproductive Rights
Athena Liu, University of Hong Kong

Medicine, Law and Social Change
Leanna Darvall, La Trobe University

Abortion Regimes
Kerry A. Petersen, La Trobe University

Human In Vitro Fertilization: A Case Study in the Regulation of Medical Innovation
Jennifer Gunning, Agricultural and Food Research Council and
Veronica English, Human Fertilisation and Embryology Authority

Law Reform and Medical Injury Litigation
Edited by *Sheila A.M. McLean,* University of Glasgow

Legal Issues in Obstetrics
Vivienne Harpwood, Cardiff Law School

Competence to Consent to Medical Treatment
John Devereux, Griffith University

Death, Dying and the Law
Edited by *Sheila A.M. McLean,* University of Glasgow

**The Contractual Reallocation of Procreative Resources and Parental Rights:
The Natural Endowment Critique**
William Joseph Wagner, The Catholic University of America

Clinical Resource Allocation: The Principles of Managed Care
Christopher Heginbotham, Riverside Mental Health Trust, London

Designer Babies
Robert Lee, Cardiff Law School and *Derek Morgan,* Cardiff Law School

Contemporary Issues in Law, Medicine and Ethics
Edited by *Sheila A.M. McLean,* University of Glasgow

Medical Negligence Law: Seeking a Balance
Andrew Fulton Phillips, University of Strathclyde

Pharmaceuticals and the European Community
Edited by *K. Collins* and *Sheila A.M. McLean,* University of Glasgow

All titles are provisional

THE ALLOCATION OF HEALTH CARE RESOURCES

An Ethical Evaluation of the 'QALY' Approach

JOHN McKIE*
JEFF RICHARDSON†
PETER SINGER*
HELGA KUHSE*

*Centre for Human Bioethics, Monash University

†National Centre for Health Program Evaluation,
Austin and Repatriation Medical Centre, Melbourne

Ashgate

DARTMOUTH

Aldershot • Brookfield USA • Singapore • Sydney

Published by
Dartmouth Publishing Company Limited
Ashgate Publishing Limited
Gower House
Croft Road
Aldershot
Hants GU11 3HR
England

Ashgate Publishing Company
Old Post Road
Brookfield
Vermont 05036
USA

British Library Cataloguing in Publication Data
The allocation of health care resources : an ethical
    evaluation of the 'Qaly' approach
    1.Health care rationing – Moral and ethical aspects
    I.McKie, John
    174.2'6

Library of Congress Cataloging-in-Publication Data
The allocation of health care resources : an ethical evaluation of the
    'QALY' approach / John McKie ... [et al.].
        p.   cm. — (Medico-legal series)
    Includes bibliographical references and index.
    ISBN 1-85521-953-0 (hb)
    1. Health care rationing.   2. Quality of life.   3. Life
expectancy.   I. McKie, John.   II. Series.
RA410.5.A455   1998   97–42927
362.1—dc21   CIP

ISBN 1 85521 953 0

Typeset by Manton Typesetters, 5–7 Eastfield Road, Louth, Lincolnshire, UK.

Printed in Great Britain by Galliard (Printers) Ltd, Great Yarmouth

Contents

List of Tables and Figures vii
Acknowledgments ix

1 Introduction **1**

2 The Background to the QALY **15**
 The Nature of Economic Evaluation 15
 Three Types of Economic Evaluation 17
  Cost–benefit analysis 17
  Cost–effectiveness analysis 21
  Cost–utility analysis and the QALY 22
 Including Quality of Life 24
 Measuring QALYs 25
 Types of QALYs 30
 Whose Preferences? 32
  Patients 33
  Health professionals 34
  The general public 35
  Mixed strategies 37
  Stated and revealed preferences 37
 Ethical Underpinning 38

3 Age Discrimination **47**
 The 'Fair Innings' Argument 48
 Eliminating Ageism? 51
 Maximizing QALYs and Maximizing Utility 52
 The Prudential Lifespan Approach 55
 Four Problems for the QALY Approach 59
  A slippery slope 59
  Utility and fairness 60
  Rival foundations 61
  Social hijacking 62
 Saving Lives versus Maximizing QALYs 64

4   Quality of Life   **73**
QALY Levels and QALY Gains   74
Money for the Rich   75
The Compensation Objection   79
The Equity Objection   81
The Need Objection   83
   The moral arbitrariness of ill health   84
   Needs, benefits and impartiality   85
   Sacrifices and complaints   87
   Reconciling need and efficiency   89
The 'Safety Net' Objection   91

5   Double Jeopardy   **99**
Random Allocation   101
The Equal Value of Lives   103
The Veil of Ignorance   104
   The purpose of the veil   105
   Slavery as a counter-example   106
   Rawls's derivation of the difference principle   107
Rational Choice and Likelihood   109
   Equal chances and unequal gains   109
   'Eligibility' for survival   111
   Identity behind the veil   114

6   Public Opinion   **117**
An Australian Survey   118
Public Opinion, Ethics and Economic Evaluation   127
A Role for the Expert Committee   128

7   Conclusion   **133**

Bibliography   135

Index   147

List of Tables and Figures

Tables

2.1 Alternative economic analyses for health and health care
    evaluation   18
2.2 Quality-adjusted life year (QALY) of competing therapies:
    some tentative estimates   23
2.3 Some utilities for health states   29
6.1 Response to each issue and difficulty of choice   121

Figures

4.1 Comparative QALY gains of Nora and Agnes before and
    after treatment   74
4.2 Comparative QALY gains of Herbert and Waldo before
    and after treatment   77

Acknowledgments

Chapter 3 draws heavily on our previously published article, 'Allocating Health Care by QALYs: The Relevance of Age', *Cambridge Quarterly Journal of Healthcare Ethics*, **5**, (4), Fall 1996, 534–45. Our thanks to the Editors of the *Cambridge Quarterly Journal of Healthcare Ethics* and the publisher, Cambridge University Press, for their kind permission to make substantial use of this article.

Our thanks also to John Harris and the Editor of the *Journal of Medical Ethics* for their kind permission to use material from the following two articles: John Harris, 'Double jeopardy and the veil of ignorance – A reply', *Journal of Medical Ethics*, **21**, (3), June 1995, 151–7; John Harris, 'Would Aristotle have played Russian Roulette?', *Journal of Medical Ethics*, **22**, (4), August 1996, 209–15. These articles formed part of a debate, conducted with us during 1995 and 1996, about the merits of the QALY approach to health care allocation. We also thank the Editor of the *Journal of Medical Ethics* for allowing us to use material from our previously published articles: 'Double jeopardy and the use of QALYs in health care allocation', *Journal of Medical Ethics*, **21**, (3), June 1995, 144–50; 'Double jeopardy, the equal value of lives and the veil of ignorance: A rejoinder to Harris', *Journal of Medical Ethics*, **22**, (4), August 1996, 204–8; 'Another peep behind the veil', *Journal of Medical Ethics*, **22**, (4), August 1996, 216–21. This debate forms part of Chapter 5.

Chapter 6 also draws heavily on, and Table 6.1 is reproduced from, *Social Science and Medicine*, **41**, (10), Erik Nord, Jeff Richardson, Andrew Street, Helga Kuhse and Peter Singer, 'Maximising Health Benefits vs Egalitarianism: An Australian Survey of Health Issues', 1429–37, Copyright 1995, with kind permission from Elsevier Science Limited, The Boulevard, Langford Lane, Kidlington OX5 1GB.

Table 2.2 comes from A. Maynard, 'Developing the health care market', *Economic Journal*, **101**, 1991, 1277–86. Table 2.3 is reprinted with permission from *Journal of Chronic Diseases*, **40**, (6), George W. Torrance, 'Utility approach to measuring health related quality of life', 593–600, 1987, Elsevier Science Inc. Our thanks to the authors of these articles and the Editors of the journal for their kind permission to reproduce the tables.

This book had its genesis in 1993, when researchers from the National Centre for Health Program Evaluation (then based at Fairfield Hospital in Melbourne), the Centre for Human Bioethics at Monash University and the National Institute of Public Health in Oslo began a study of community attitudes towards resource allocation practices in the health sector, and the ethical foundations of those practices. We would like to thank the National Health and Medical Research Council for awarding to Helga Kuhse and Peter Singer the grant that supported this research.

1 Introduction

Can we place a monetary value on a human life? Many people reject the very idea of doing so. How could we possibly arrive at any figure that would represent the value of a human life? And even if we could, would that not be a crass attempt to convert to money values something that is, quite literally, beyond any price? What would we think of a society that, after spending a certain amount in attempting to save the lives of miners trapped after an underground mishap, said that it had reached the limit of the value of the miners' lives, and left them to die rather than spend more on rescuing them?

Yet we do live in a society that allows people to die when it costs too much to save them. It happens all the time, in areas like road safety, workplace safety, overseas aid and – the subject of this book – in health care. In every society there are limited budgets for these matters, and spending more could save more lives. In many cases we even know roughly how much it would be necessary to spend to save another life. Overseas aid undoubtedly offers the least expensive way of saving lives, since providing very basic medical care can save large numbers of lives in developing countries. The fact that we do not do this implies that we value the lives of members of our own society far more highly than we value the lives of members of other societies. Although this is a major ethical issue, it is not the one with which this volume is concerned. Henceforth we focus on decisions about the value of the lives of members of our own society, and leave problems about the international allocation of resources to one side.

Road accident statistics enable us to identify a country's 10 most dangerous intersections. Suppose that they tell us that, if nothing is done about these intersections, 60 people will lose their lives at them over the next five years. We also know that it would cost $100 million to modify all of these intersections to bring them up to the safety standards of other, less dangerous intersections. We could then expect that, instead of 60 deaths over the next five years, there would only be 10 deaths. If we do not allocate the funds to do this, we are saying that we are not willing to spend $2 million to save a human life. We do not know, from these facts, what the implicit value of a human life in this society is, but we know that it is less than $2 million. In fact, since the modifications would presumably reduce the much larger number of non-fatal accidents as well, and we would surely be willing to spend something to do that, the implicit value of a human life in this imaginary scenario would be significantly less than $2 million. We have also taken no account of the value of the lives saved over a longer period than five years. But the details are not important here. This is an imaginary example, and the figures would vary from country to country, but it is not an unrealistic example.

In the same way, a financial limit on our efforts to save human life is present in every national health care budget. We may know that providing better screening to detect the early stages of some forms of cancer would save a specific number of lives, and yet often we do not do it because the cost is too high. This is generally also true of the amount we allocate to intensive care. Providing more intensive care beds in our major hospitals would, over a year, save some lives, but intensive care beds require a high staff/patient ratio and so cost a lot of money. The budgets that each society sets in various areas implicitly place monetary values on human lives, although it is not necessarily the same value in each area. These budgets say that it is not worth spending a larger amount, even when it is clear that, if this larger amount was spent, more lives would be saved.

Are we then in the position of the society that allows entombed miners to die because the costs of rescuing them are too high? One difference is that, in the case of the miners, we know who the victims are. We can more easily identify with them, and they will presumably have families and friends who will be distraught at their peril, and desperate for their rescue. In contrast, we do not know, when we set our road safety budget, who will be killed at dangerous intersections during the coming year (although we will be able to find out, as the year unfolds, who we might have saved). In the case of cancer screening programmes, we do not know when we make the decision who will be affected by our decision not to fund the programme, and we may never be able to find out, because some of these cancers may prove fatal no matter when they are detected.

This difference is psychologically significant. To abandon identifiable people to certain death when they could be saved appears to be a more heartless decision, and to symbolize a lack of concern for human life to a far greater degree, than a failure to reduce the road toll. On reflection, however, it is hard to place much moral weight on this psychological difference. Those killed in car crashes on dangerous intersections, and those who die from preventable cancers, will themselves be people who are no less real than the trapped miners, and their families will grieve no less for their deaths.

Still, as we have said, every society sets some limits on how much it will spend to save lives; and while we may well think that present limits are too low, it can hardly be denied that there have to be such limits. Otherwise, in the end, we would have to stop spending money on everything else we value – including education, the preservation of wilderness, and cultural pursuits – in order to increase our chances of saving one more life. Such a decision would be difficult to justify. Life is a great good, but is it the only good? Without life, we cannot experience any of those goods, such as pleasure, aesthetic appreciation or friendship, that require the existence of a subject capable of experiences. But if being honoured after one's death is a good, then there are some goods that can accrue to people after they die, and so being alive is not a precondition of *all* goods. Paradoxical as the notion may seem, many people have, rightly or wrongly, chosen death before dishonour.

In any case, putting aside tricky philosophical questions about whether good things can happen to you after you die, there is a difference between preferring some other good to life itself, and rejecting all other goods in order to avoid a small *risk* of losing one's life. We all do things that involve a slight but measurable risk of death in order to do other things we value. We drive to the beach, or board a plane to go to a conference, when we could be sitting safely at home. So our own behaviour strongly suggests that, while we think life is a great good, we do not think that it is the only good. We can therefore ask: *how* great a good is it? What should we be prepared to give up for it, and what should we not be prepared to give up?

This is the most fundamental ethical question in the debate over the allocation of health care resources. There are, however, some who think that it is a mistake to ask how much we, as a society, should spend on health care. Instead, they say that we should leave this decision to every individual member of society. Individuals can decide for themselves, they say, how much health care they wish to buy. In a free market for health care insurance (including, under this label, health maintenance schemes), providers will compete by offering various levels of service at appropriate prices. If you want to spend half your income on a blue-ribbon scheme to ensure that you receive the absolute best in health care whenever you need it, you will be able to do so. If, on the other hand, you prefer to spend most of your income on other things and take your chances with whatever kind of treatment you can afford at the time you happen to fall ill, you will be under no compulsion to buy any health insurance at all. Such an arrangement, its advocates claim, eliminates paternalistic coercion by the state, and maximizes freedom of choice.

One obvious objection to this proposal is that some people will be unable to buy an adequate level of health care insurance, no matter how high a proportion of their income they would like to put into it, simply because they earn so little that, after providing for the necessities of life, there is not enough left. Thus a free market allocation of health care resources will mean that some people die because they are unable to afford the most basic health care services, such as calling a doctor when they are seriously ill.

Some opponents of state paternalism acknowledge the injustice in the existing distribution of income. They seek to remedy this, and yet still maximize freedom of choice, by suggesting that we provide everyone with a guaranteed minimum income, leaving them free to spend it as they wish. But while this may go some way towards providing a more just distribution of income, it does not solve the problem of people dying because they cannot pay for basic health services. For among those receiving the guaranteed minimum income there would be some who would prudently set aside a proportion of it for health insurance, and others who would do no such thing. A few would even gamble it away or spend it on alcohol. Tough-minded defenders of individual choice might feel that such people should face the consequences of their choices, even if that means that they are left to die outside the doors of our hospitals. But are there any who are so hard-hearted as to believe that the children of these gamblers and alcoholics should meet the same fate?

If we, as a community, find it unacceptable to allow our fellow-citizens – and their children – to die from diseases that could easily be cured by medical treatments available at modest cost to most members of society, we cannot avoid some community involvement in health care and we must ask how much we, as a society, should spend on it.

The discussion that follows begins with the assumption that a society has allocated a certain quantity of resources to health care. In doing so, the society will have answered, whether deliberately or (more probably) haphazardly and without fully realizing what it is doing, the fundamental question of how much it is prepared to spend to save a human life. Now a further and scarcely less significant ethical question arises: given that we have a finite health care budget, how can we best spend it? This book is a contribution towards the search for an answer to this question. It does not attempt to answer it by giving concrete spending suggestions. We are not in a position to say that it is better to spend our money on, say, preventive health services rather than intensive care units. Before such specific proposals can even be discussed in a fruitful way, we need to have a clear understanding of what we mean by a 'better' way of spending our money. Is it, for example, better to distribute health care resources as *equally* as possible, so that everyone gets the same amount? Or should we seek to distribute the resources so that they will bring about the *greatest benefits*? The issue rapidly appears to become a choice between justice and utility. But is it really? Are justice and utility incompatible here? These are deep ethical questions, with a long history. Before we go further into them it will be helpful to distinguish between different kinds of ethical questions.

The questions we are considering are general theoretical questions about the kinds of goals we should pursue. To answer them we need to think critically about what we value most. Is the ultimate goal the welfare of all human beings, or perhaps of all sentient beings? Or are there some things, for example some forms of injustice, that are wrong in themselves, irrespective of their consequences? These are issues in what is usually known as 'normative ethics'. But what kind of a discussion are we having, when we discuss what our goals ought to be, and whether some things are wrong irrespective of their consequences? Is there something that we are seeking to know, in much the same way as we may seek knowledge of how to live to a ripe old age? Is it possible to discover objective values, or objective rules of conduct? Or are we discussing a field in which we can only state our preferences, as we may do when discussing our gastronomic tastes, or perhaps our ranking of the paintings of one artist above those of another? These questions take us into the realm of 'meta-ethics', a part of the philosophical discussion of ethics that includes questions about, rather than within, normative ethics. Because much of this book is a discussion of ethical issues, it may be worthwhile at this point to say something about the nature of ethics itself.

Since ancient Greek times there have been thinkers who have denounced ethics as in some way a fraud or deception. The Greek sophist Thrasymachus, for example, is portrayed by Plato in his *Republic* as claiming that what we call 'just' simply represents the interests of the stronger: in other words, that our ideas of right and wrong are imposed on us by those with the power to do so, for their own advantage. More than two thousand years later, Karl Marx sometimes appeared to take a similar view, when he suggested that all morality is 'class morality' and that, in a capitalist society, the dominant moral ideas will serve the needs of the capitalist economy. Friedrich Nietzsche argued for the mirror image of Thrasymachus's idea – namely, that ethics, or more specifically, Christian ethics, are imposed on the strong by the masses of weak people, to prevent them realizing their heroic strengths (Nietzsche, 1955). But these thinkers who protest about the allegedly fraudulent nature of particular moralities only serve to show the inescapability of morality as such, since, if there were no such thing as morality, fraud itself would be nothing to be concerned about. Nor is the condemnation of fraud the only moral view that such thinkers hold, explicitly or implicitly. No one who has read the chapter of *Capital* in which Marx describes the sweatshops of 19th-century England can mistake his powerful sense of moral outrage at a system that builds the wealth of the few on the misery of so many.

If we cannot, without self-contradiction, denounce morality as a fraud, can we say that it is nevertheless entirely a matter of subjective judgment, and therefore nothing that we can argue about? This is also a view with a long history. Early subjectivists believed that to say an action is right is merely to say that one has a positive feeling towards it, whereas to say that an action is wrong is to say that one has a negative feeling about it. But this view was liable to a fatal objection: it implies that, when A says that an action is wrong, and B says that the same action is right, they are not really disagreeing. For each is simply describing his or her attitude, and it is clearly true that they have different attitudes. The situation should be similar to A saying 'Coffee keeps me awake at night' and B saying 'I fall asleep as soon as my head hits the pillow, no matter how much coffee I drink.' The expression of contrary moral judgments, however, is not simply a matter of two compatible descriptions; it is a disagreement, often the most serious kind of disagreement that there can be, and any analysis of the nature of moral judgment must be able to account for this fact.

In the mid-20th century, a more sophisticated form of subjectivism, known as emotivism, was formulated. It avoided the objection just discussed by denying that moral judgments describe anything at all. Instead, the emotivists said, they are used to express emotions or attitudes. On this view, to say 'euthanasia is wrong' does not state any facts about euthanasia, not even the fact that the speaker has a negative attitude to euthanasia. It is, crudely put, rather as if one had said: 'Euthanasia, Boo!' Conversely, those who say that euthanasia is justifiable are saying 'Euthanasia, Hurrah!'. On this account it is easier to understand why people on different sides of a moral issue should feel that they are in disagreement with each other, for that is certainly how the rival groups of supporters feel at a football match as they barrack each other's teams. But while the problem of explaining why there is disagreement in ethics may thus be solved by emotivism, there is still something unsatisfactory about this analysis. Football supporters generally do not try to convince supporters of other teams that they should switch their allegiances. They may explain why they support the team they follow – for example, by saying that they grew up near its home ground, or their Dad always followed it – but they do not pretend that these are reasons for everyone to follow that team. Moral disagreement therefore remains different from the disagreement between the supporters of rival football teams, and the difference lies in the nature of the reasons that we use, or try to use, to defend our moral views. They are reasons that, we feel, should be persuasive to everyone.

Before we explore the implications of this account of the role that reason plays in moral dispute, there is one other popular view of the nature of ethics that needs to be mentioned. Many people reject subjectivism on the grounds that it is not individual attitudes that determine what is right or wrong, but the attitudes of the culture in which we live. In the 19th century, anthropologists came to know many different cultures, and found that the people of those cultures had ethical views very different from those that were standardly taken for granted in European society. This led some anthropologists and others to hold that, since morality is relative to culture, no culture can have any basis for regarding its morality as superior to any other culture. Although this view may seem like a much-needed weapon against western cultural imperialism, it has implications that few would want to embrace. Again, some of these implications relate to the nature of moral disagreement. Relativism is like subjectivism writ large. For a relativist, when people from two different cultures appear to disagree about an ethical issue, they are really each just reporting the views of their own culture. Hence, if these cultures do in fact have different views on the issue, there is really no disagreement, there can be no resolution, and it is impossible to say that one is right and the other is wrong. Bearing in mind that some cultures have practised slavery, or the burning of widows on the funeral pyre of their husbands, this is hard to accept.

A more promising alternative to all of the meta-ethical views mentioned so far is universal prescriptivism, an approach to ethics developed by the Oxford philosopher R.M. Hare (1963; 1981). Hare shares with the emotivists the premise that ethical judgments do not state facts and hence are not true or false in the ordinary sense that descriptive statements may be true or false in virtue of the accuracy of their descriptions. Instead, he classifies ethical judgments as a form of imperative or, more specifically, as prescriptions. Ethical judgments prescribe conduct. But Hare parts company with emotivists in the role he allows for reasoning in ethics. This role is made possible by the claim that ethical judgments form a special family of prescriptions, namely universal prescriptions. It is important to be clear about exactly what this means. It does not mean that ethical judgments are exceptionless moral rules, such as 'Never tell a lie'. On the contrary, on Hare's view, ethical judgments can be very specifically tailored to particular circumstances. But ethical judgments are, Hare claims, universalizable in the sense that, if I make an ethical judgment, I must be prepared to state it in universal terms and apply it to all relevantly similar situations. The requirement that the judgment be stated in 'universal terms' means that it must be possible to formulate it in a way that avoids such things as proper names or personal pronouns. A judgment that tax avoidance is wrong unless I am the one who avoids paying tax is not a universalizable judgment, although a judgment that tax avoidance is wrong unless the tax avoided is used to save the lives of people dying from hunger would be. A universalizable judgment cannot be based on the role that I play – or, in particular, whether I benefit or lose by the action that is being judged.

The universal aspect of ethical judgments forms a bridge between meta-ethical analysis of the meanings of moral terms and normative moral argument. Given that ethical judgments must be universalizable, whenever I purport to make an ethical judgment I can be challenged to put myself in the position of the parties affected and see if I would still be able to accept that judgment. Suppose, for example, that I own a small factory and the cheapest way for me to get rid of some waste is to pour it into a nearby river. I do not take water from this river, but I know that some villagers living downstream do and the waste may make them ill. The requirement that ethical judgments should be universalizable will make it impossible for me to justify my conduct because, if I were to put myself in the position of the villagers, I would not accept that the profits of the factory owner should outweigh the risk of adverse effects on my health and that of my children. In this way universalizability provides a basis for an element of reasoning in ethical deliberation. It also requires us to take into account the interests and preferences of others affected by our actions. Since the rightness or wrongness of our actions will, on this view, depend on the way in which they affect others, Hare's universal prescriptivism leads to a form of consequentialism; that is, the view that the rightness of an action depends on its consequences.

An influential contemporary rival to Hare's approach to ethics is that taken by John Rawls, a professor of philosophy at Harvard University, in his book, *A Theory of Justice* (1971). It is known as 'reflective equilibrium'. Instead of searching for a single foundation on which a theory of ethics can be built, Rawls says that ethical theory must start with our ordinary moral convictions – in other words, our intuitions. An ethical theory should aim to match our moral universe by being consistent with as many of these intuitions as possible, in much the same way as a scientific theory aims to explain the natural universe by being consistent with as many of the observable phenomena as possible. When the ethical theory is an inherently plausible one, but does not match all of our moral intuitions, we may rely on the theory itself as a basis for jettisoning some intuitions. This approach is thus a form of intuitionism, in that in the end our moral intuitions are the testing ground of our moral theories. It is a modified form of intuitionism, though, because our intuitions are not sacrosanct. They are liable to criticism and rejection if they do not match an otherwise plausible ethical theory that explains most, but not all, of our intuitions. Hence the term 'reflective equilibrium', the idea being that we should reach an equilibrium between our initial moral intuitions, and the ethical theory that seeks to harmonize them. This approach combines elements of cultural relativism with the objectivism of reason. It does not necessarily lead us to a single 'true' moral theory, because different cultures may have different sets of intuitions and so may reach a different point of reflective equilibrium.

Let us then turn our attention to normative ethics. We have already seen that Hare's view leads to a form of consequentialism. The most fundamental divide in normative ethics is between consequentialists and those who defend the view that there are some things which it would always be wrong to do, no matter what the consequences. The most eloquent portrayal of this fundamental divide comes from Dostoevsky's *The Karamazov Brothers*:

> ... imagine that you are charged with building the edifice of human destiny, the ultimate aim of which is to bring people happiness, to give them peace and contentment at last, but that in order to achieve this it is essential and unavoidable to torture just one little speck of creation, that same little child beating her chest with her little fists, and imagine that this edifice has to be erected on her unexpiated tears. Would you agree to be the architect under those conditions? Tell me honestly! (Vol. I, Pt 2, Bk 5, Ch. 4)

This view, that some things are always wrong, no matter what their consequences, has for most of western history been the prevailing approach to morality, at least at the level of what has been officially taught and approved by the institutions of church and state. The Ten Commandments of the Hebrew scriptures served as a model for much of the Christian era, and the Roman Catholic church built up an elaborate system of morality based on rules to which no exceptions were allowed.

Another example of an ethic of rules is that of Immanuel Kant (1948). Kant's ethic is based on his 'categorical imperative', which he states in several distinct formulations. One is that we must always act so that we can will the maxim of our action to be a universal law. This can be interpreted as a form of Hare's idea of universalizability, which we have already encountered. Another is that we must always treat other people as ends, never as means. While these formulations of the categorical imperative might be applied in various ways (including Hare's consequentialism), in Kant's hands they lead to inviolable rules, for example against making promises that we do not intend to keep. Kant thought that it was always wrong to tell a lie. In response to a critic who suggested that this rule has exceptions, Kant said that it would be wrong to lie even if someone had taken refuge in your house and a person seeking to murder him came to your door and asked if you knew where he was. Modern Kantians often reject this hardline approach to rules and claim that Kant's categorical imperative did not require him to hold so strictly to the rule against lying.

At the opposite extreme to such rule-based approaches to ethics is utilitarianism, the classic form of consequentialism which was developed by the English philosopher and political reformer Jeremy Bentham in the late 18th and early 19th centuries. Bentham held that an action is right if it leads to a greater surplus of happiness over misery than any possible alternative, and wrong if it does not. By 'greater surplus of happiness', Bentham and later utilitarians had in mind the idea of adding up all the pleasure or happiness that resulted from the action and subtracting from that total all the pain or misery to which the action gave rise. Naturally, in some circumstances, it might only be possible to reduce misery, and then the right action should be understood as the one that will result in less misery than any possible alternative.

The utilitarian view is striking in many ways. It puts forward a single principle that it claims can provide the right answer to any ethical dilemma, if only we can predict what the consequences of our actions will be. It takes ethics down from the mysterious realm of duties and rules, and bases ethical decisions on something that almost everyone understands and values. And its single principle is applied universally, without fear or favour. Bentham said: 'Everybody to count for one, nobody for more than one', by which he meant that the happiness of a common tramp counted for as much as that of a noble, and the happiness of an African was no less important than that of a European.

Many 20th century consequentialists agree with Bentham to the extent that they think the rightness or wrongness of an action must depend on its consequences, but they have abandoned the idea that maximizing net happiness is the ultimate goal. Instead, they argue that we should seek to bring about whatever will satisfy the greatest number of desires or preferences. This variation, which is known as 'preference utilitarianism', does not regard anything as good, except in so far as it is wanted or desired. More intense or strongly held preferences would get more weight than weak preferences. As we are about to see, preference utilitarianism lies behind one of the most important answers to the question of how we decide that one way of using our limited health care resources is better than another.

Critics of preference utilitarianism argue that it implies that, if a sadist desires to torture an innocent victim, the desire of the sadist is weighed along with that of the victim, and if it is stronger, torture would be right. Preference utilitarians respond that a sadist's desire to torture someone will never be as strong as the intended victim's desire not to be tortured. Critics still argue that, if there are enough sadists who want to see the victim tortured, their preferences will surely outweigh that of the victim, and that this is unjust. At this point utilitarians usually appeal to the greater long-term preference satisfaction that will come about if we discourage people from having desires that require others to suffer.

John Stuart Mill, the most famous of Bentham's philosophical descendants, tried to handle the possibility of a conflict between justice and the maximization of happiness by suggesting that, since we often do not have the time or ability to calculate the consequences of each individual decision, we should rely on general rules that will in most circumstances produce the best results. Thus the rules of justice, he urged, are those that in the long run will lead to greater happiness than any alternative set of rules.

In the 20th century, some utilitarians adopted a view reminiscent of Mill's as a means of dealing with the objection that following utilitarianism would mean lying, stealing and breaking promises, whenever so doing would bring about more good than telling the truth, being honest or keeping promises. This objection could be met in either of two ways. The more tough-minded utilitarians met it by arguing that in most circumstances the value of upholding the social conventions of truth telling, honesty and promise keeping would outweigh the advantages of acting contrary to the usual moral rules and, when this is not the case, it is better that the rules should be broken. This group became known as 'act-utilitarians' because they continued to insist that the utilitarian test of right and wrong be applied to every act we choose to perform. Other utilitarians considered that the act-utilitarian response was either not convincing in itself or left open too many situations in which breaking the rules remained, on balance, the right thing to do. They argued that instead of asking of each act whether it maximized the good, we should ask this question of the rules over time. Then, once we have decided which rules would, if widely followed, lead to the best consequences, we should judge acts right or wrong on the basis of whether they conform to those rules. Hence this latter group became known as rule-utilitarians.

Rule-utilitarianism was immediately faced with the problem of trying to define how specific a rule could be. At one extreme, we might try to obey short and simple rules like 'Do not lie' or 'Keep your promises'. But even in everyday life, most people recognize some exceptions to these rules, for example where telling a lie might save a life. So rule-utilitarians might modify the rule so that it reads: 'Do not lie except to save a life'. But is this the only exception? Why is it not right to tell a lie to prevent serious injury to someone? And so the questions go on, pushing the rule-utilitarian in the direction of more and more specific rules. The problem is that, if the rule-utilitarian allows exceptions to rules whenever it would, all things considered, lead to better consequences than not allowing an exception, the difference between act- and rule-utilitarianism has effectively disappeared.

R.M. Hare advocates a normative ethic that is neither act- nor rule-utilitarianism, but incorporates some features of both. We should adopt rules for everyday moral decision making, he urges, because to try to calculate the consequences of every act is barely feasible and, if it were, we would still be in danger of being led astray by particular emotions or biases that might influence our calculation. With the rule-utilitarian, Hare would say that the rules we choose should be those that have been shown over time to have good consequences. On the other hand, there may be rare occasions when we can be quite sure that, because of some special features of our situation, following the usual rules will have worse consequences than breaking them. Then Hare agrees with the act-utilitarian that it is pointless to obey the rule just for the sake of obeying it. Instead, we should do what will bring about the best consequences.

Some normative positions lie between a strict ethic of rules and a utilitarian ethic that judges everything by its consequences. Early in the 20th century, W.D. Ross developed an ethic based on prima facie duties (Ross, 1930). According to Ross, we have several distinct duties, for example a duty of justice and a duty of beneficence. Ross said that these duties are prima facie in the sense that none of them makes an absolute claim on us. In any particular situation, we may be under different prima facie duties, and they may conflict. We may owe a duty of gratitude to someone which will lead us to do a favour to that person; but if we do so we may be unable to act beneficently to someone else. What is the right thing to do, all things considered, will then be a decision that we reach after weighing up the stringency of the various duties we are under, as they apply to the particular situation we are in. Each applicable duty must be given some weight, but will not necessarily prevail. Since the duty of beneficence requires us to do good in general, Ross's ethic is in effect a balancing of the utilitarian view with a number of other widely held moral beliefs about what we should do. It is therefore closer to conventional moral views than a pure utilitarian view, while remaining less rigid than an ethic of moral rules to which no exceptions are allowed. Despite this, support for Ross's ethic of prima facie duties has dwindled in the second half of the 20th century. One major weakness is its reliance on intuition – both at the level of selecting the duties themselves and then in weighing them up in specific situations. Since other people have different intuitions, it is not plausible to maintain that these matters are self-evident. Why, then, should one set of intuitions be preferred to any other? And why, in a particular situation, should one way of weighing up intuitions be chosen over any other? Without answers to these questions, the ethic of prima facie duties fails to give sufficient direction.

An approach to ethics based on rights, rather than duties, can either be absolute, like an ethic of rules, or prima facie, like Ross's ethic. Everything depends on whether the rights are regarded as absolutely inviolable, no matter what, or as something that must be taken into account, but can be overridden in certain circumstances. When rights are made the basis of ethics, however, the problems that we have just seen in respect of Ross's ethic of duties are likely also to be present: that is, different people have different views about what rights individuals have, and what to do when they clash. Moreover, an ethic of rights is incomplete, in that there are many things we ought to do which go beyond respecting rights, for example helping strangers in need. Most philosophers see rights, not as the basis of ethics, but as derivative from more fundamental ethical principles. Rights are commonly based on Kantian views of the importance of individual autonomy, and the requirement that we always treat people as ends rather than as means. At the social or political level, rights can also be derived from utilitarian views. John Stuart Mill, for example, was both a utilitarian and a strong advocate of limits to the authority of the state, because he believed that when the state interferes with the individual – except where necessary to prevent harm to others – it often interferes wrongly. Moreover, without freedom of expression, Mill thought that we can never be sure that the truth will emerge, and without freedom for individuals to experiment with different ways of living, we are less likely to make social progress.

John Rawls, whose approach to the possibilities of argument in ethics combines, as we saw earlier, both intuition and reason, has developed an account of justice that has influenced many thinkers in the second half of the 20th century. He suggests that we can reach sound principles of justice by asking what principles people would agree to if they had to meet under an imaginary 'veil of ignorance' that would prevent them from knowing what particular characteristics each of them had. This is a social contract model of ethics, reminiscent of the 17th-century philosopher John Locke, but with the twist that the contracting parties do not know if they are black or white, male or female, rich or poor, religious or atheist, gifted in various ways, or in none at all. Rawls thinks that under these circumstances people would choose two basic principles of justice. The first would ensure the maximum liberty for all, compatible with the like liberty being granted to others; and the second would provide for equal opportunity and for a distribution of the society's resources designed to raise the minimum level of welfare in the community to the highest possible. This last idea – known as 'maximin' because it directs us to maximize the minimum level of welfare – has attracted many people, because to them it seems fair that we should try to help the worst-off before we help those who are better off. However, others have pointed out that, treated as an absolute rule, it could lead to some unattractive outcomes. For example, suppose that in a society in which everyone is at an equal, but rather miserable, level of welfare, it somehow became possible to raise 99 per cent of the members of the society to a very high level of welfare, but at the cost of making the remaining 1 per cent just a tiny bit worse off, to an extent that they would only barely notice. This would be ruled out by maximin. Of course, opinions will differ on whether this is, or is not, an objection to maximin. Utilitarians will think it absurd to prohibit conferring so great a benefit on the overwhelming majority of the society in order to prevent so small a loss for the remainder. Some others may think that it is the right answer.

In conclusion, let us return to Dostoevsky's challenge. How would a utilitarian answer it? If answering honestly – and if one really could be certain that this was a sure way, and the only way, of bringing lasting happiness to all the people of the world – utilitarians would have to say yes, they would accept the task of being the architect of the happiness of the world at the cost of the child's unexpiated tears. For they would point out that the suffering of that child, wholly undeserved as it is, will be repeated a millionfold over the next century, for other children, just as innocent, who are victims of starvation, disease and brutality. So if this one child must be sacrificed to stop all this suffering then, terrible as it is, the child must be sacrificed.

Fantasy apart, there can be no architect of the happiness of the world. The world is too big and complex a place for that. But there can be architects of the happiness of specific sub-groups of people in particular places and circumstances. Those who allocate health care resources are architects of the happiness – or perhaps more accurately, of the reduction of suffering – of the patients who will be affected by their decisions. The ethical questions that we have been considering here will therefore find their echo in the discussion that follows.

2 The Background to the QALY

The Nature of Economic Evaluation

Economic evaluation is concerned with the costs and benefits of programmes or projects and with the distributional effects of these. In principle, both costs and benefits are broad concepts and far broader than the common misconception that they refer only to money. 'Benefits' may encompass any consequences of a project that are relevant to human well-being. Costs (or 'opportunity costs') refer to the value of any opportunity or benefit forgone because of resources used by the project. The cost of buying this book is a certain number of dollars, or pounds, or whatever the currency may be. The opportunity cost of buying it is whatever else you could have bought with those pounds or dollars. Once you have bought the book, it will not cost you any more money to read it, though reading it still carries an opportunity cost. The opportunity cost of reading this book is the forgone opportunity of carrying out some other activity: reading another book, earning income or enjoying leisure time. Clearly, opportunity costs only arise because resources are finite. Without this constraint every desirable activity could be carried out and there would be no need for economic evaluation. Conceptually the most fundamental rule of economic evaluation, that benefits must exceed costs, may therefore be translated as the dictum that to be worthwhile the benefits arising from a project must be greater than the benefits lost because of the project. 'Benefit–cost analysis' could easily be relabelled 'benefit–benefit analysis.'

In principle, costs and benefits construed in this broad way could be said to subsume any relevant distributional effects arising from the project. If the direct costs of a project (for example, payments to doctors and hospitals) fall disproportionately and unfairly upon some individual or group then the loss of well-being because of this unfairness could be considered a further cost. Similarly, if material benefits (for example, improvements in health status) are very unequally distributed, as a result of which there is general dissatisfaction with the inequity, this also could be considered a cost. In practice, distributional issues are almost invariably measured and evaluated separately because of the difficulty in finding a unit of measurement which includes both distributional concerns, on the one hand, and costs and benefits on the other.[1]

It is, of course, difficult to quantify – or even to enumerate – all of the possible direct and indirect effects of a project upon well-being. In practice, economic evaluation attempts to identify the quantitatively most significant effects and to devise measurement techniques for taking account of them. If there is a market for a product, its price will often suffice as a means for measuring its value. But evaluations commonly include a range of effects for which there are no market or monetary prices. Examples include the value of home duties, leisure time, travel time and environmental impact. Many of the techniques of cost–benefit analysis have arisen from the need to quantify these non-market effects. Of course, measurement of these effects is difficult, and invariably imperfect. However, the gold standard which guides measurement is – or should be – the effect upon well-being; and imperfect measurement is justified by the belief that it is better to measure the correct concepts imperfectly than the wrong concepts with great precision.

The distinctive feature of economics is its valuation of effects. Measurement of the physical effects is usually the province of some other discipline. Economists do not have the techniques needed to measure environmental degradation or air pollution. They are concerned with evaluating such effects once they have been quantified in physical terms. Similarly, there are no specifically economic techniques for evaluating the effects of a medical intervention in natural units (for example, years of life gained). Calculating the natural units is the domain of the epidemiologist or clinical scientist who will employ the random control trial, case control, experiment or laboratory-based model to derive results. Quantifying the *value* of the units is the domain of the economist who will usually employ cost–benefit, cost–effectiveness or cost–utility analysis. In brief, the benefits of a project are equal to the effects measured in natural units times the value of these units.[2]

All of these techniques were late arrivals in economics. The oldest, cost–benefit analysis (CBA), dates back to the 1930s and the most recent, cost–utility analysis (CUA), was enunciated formally in 1977 by Weinstein and Stason (see Warner and Luce, 1982). Before the development of explicit evaluation techniques, it was simply assumed that the market would determine which projects should or should not be undertaken. In the 20th century, governments have increasingly intervened in the economy because of the belief that unregulated markets often 'fail'; that is, they do not produce some outcomes that are technically possible and socially desirable. As a consequence, governments have directly produced some products, provided some services and transferred resources to achieve a more equitable distribution of income. These 'market failures' may arise because of the scale and riskiness of the project (for example, the construction of dams or large-scale irrigation projects). Alternatively, they may be a result of 'externalities': costs or benefits that are 'external' to the private economy in the sense that no money price is placed upon them, as in the case of pollution or the benefits of vaccination to those not directly vaccinated. Governments have also deemed some commodities such as health care and education to be so meritorious that they have been unwilling to leave their provision entirely to the private market.

Three Types of Economic Evaluation

Cost-Benefit Analysis

The three chief forms of economic evaluation are outlined in Table 2.1. The defining characteristic of CBA is that all of the potential benefits of health care, including the value of life, are reduced to dollars. This means that, in principle, the technique can be used to rank alternative projects within a sector but, more importantly, to compare projects across sectors: for example, in housing, education and transport. In principle it can therefore be used to determine the macro-allocation of resources to each sector: the (monetary) benefit of every project can be compared with the (monetary) opportunity cost in all other sectors, and sectorial sizes adjusted until global benefits can no longer be obtained by transferring resources from sector to sector. In practice, CBA has been widely used in the health sector (Mushkin, 1962; Klarman, 1965; Weisbrod, 1971), but macro-allocations have never been determined by CBA.[3]

The human capital approach   It has been difficult to find a satisfactory technique for determining the dollar value of a human life and for some the problem is insoluble. Two approaches have been developed. First, in the 'material welfare' tradition of Martial and Pigou, the human capital approach has treated the value of a human life as being external to the individual, and measured by the present value of their future earnings (Robinson, 1986). The human being is literally valued in the same way as productive capital. This approach, pioneered in the health sector by Mushkin (1962) and Rice and Cooper (1967), has been widely criticized for several reasons. In the first

Table 2.1   Alternative economic analyses for health and health care evaluation

Type of analysis	Benefits (outcomes) included	Defining characteristics
1 Cost–benefit analysis	Only outcomes which can be valued in dollars are included	Benefits measured exclusively in dollars
	Often excludes 'intangibles' such as alleviation of pain and suffering	Only one project needs to be considered
		Selection criterion: benefits exceed costs
2 Cost–effectiveness analysis	Only one 'dimension' of outcome is relevant, such as lives saved or cases of a disease detected	More than one project must be considered: projects are ranked
		Selection criterion: minimize cost/outcome: for example, minimize cost/life (that is, maximize lives saved/cost)
2(a) Cost minimization	Outcomes identical: for example, the same 10 lives saved with both options	More than one project must be considered: projects are ranked
		No assessment of the 'value' of outcomes as they are identical
		Selection criterion: minimize cost
3 Cost–utility analysis	Outcome is multi-dimensional	Quality of life is measured in more than one project
	Quality of life is quantitatively important	Life years are weighted to obtain 'quality-adjusted life years' (QALYs)
		Projects are 'ranked'
		Selection criterion: minimize cost/QALY (that is, maximize QALYs/cost)

place, it discriminates against those who are less productive, on grounds that are morally arbitrary. For example, in a study by Cooper and Brodie (1976) it was found that, using this approach, the 25–29-year-old white male college graduate was worth 2.8 times as much as a black high school dropout of the same age, and 11.6 times as great as a person approaching retirement. Retired persons have no human capital as defined by market values, and men are worth more than women. A second objection is that humans are generally not valued strictly for their productivity. The human capital approach places no intrinsic value upon the worth of individuals to their friends or society more generally, and thus provides an incomplete account of the value of human life.

Despite these apparently fatal objections, the human capital approach has been very widely used because of its simplicity and the availability of data. But in view of its shortcomings human capital must be rejected as a method for calculating the total value of a person. It is, at best, defensible as a measure of a person's contribution to the gross domestic product (GDP) and this is at best a sub-set of the factors determining the value of an individual life.

A third objection, often raised by economists, is that the human capital approach does not measure the strength of people's preferences. Elsewhere in the economy, the criterion of 'value' is people's preferences as revealed by what they buy in markets. It is argued that this willingness to pay is an indication of the strength of their preferences and that 'value' should reflect preferences. For this reason, many economists have argued that 'willingness to pay' is theoretically superior to human capital as a methodology for evaluating human life, and should underlie cost–benefit analysis.

The 'willingness to pay' approach The chief obstacle to implementing this approach is, of course, that there is no market in which we can observe people directly buying life. How then are we to infer the value of a life? The solution that has most commonly been adopted is to observe the amount that people are prepared to pay for a reduction in the risk of death or to observe the monetary compensation paid for an increased risk of death and to extrapolate from this to the value of life. If, for example, people are prepared to accept $10 000 in exchange for a 1 per cent increase in the risk of death, it is inferred that the value of a death to a person is $100 \times \$10\ 000 = \$1$ million. Typically, the value of the compensation needed for this risk is 'observed' econometrically by comparing the incomes received by workers exposed to different levels of risk (for example, window cleaners working on high rise buildings, firemen, policemen, and so on).[4]

The approach has produced a very wide range of estimates of the implicit value of life. In his review of the technique, Viscousi (1993) reported values as low as $US (1990) 600 000 and as high as $US (1990) 16.2 million, which suggests, as a minimum, that the results are extremely sensitive to the model and statistical technique used to elicit risk compensation. A more fundamental problem is that the process of extrapolation from the context of a low risk to the certainty of death is highly problematical. That is, it is uncertain whether it is legitimate to infer the compensation needed for high risk of death from the compensation needed for accepting a low risk. The context of the low-risk situation is quite different. Expectations, hopes, fears and anxiety will be different and people's evaluation of risk is clearly associated with these subjective factors. There has, in fact, been a significant debate over this issue and there are both theoretical grounds for doubting the validity of the inference (Richardson, 1994) and extensive evidence that the inference is empirically wrong (Schoemaker, 1982).[5] This evidence suggests that the willingness to pay studies are, at best, measuring the value of life contaminated by the value of risk.

Despite this problem, some economists argue that there is no acceptable alternative to this approach. They accept that the value of a full life cannot be revealed by people buying and selling lives as they buy and sell breakfast cereal. Furthermore, preferences must be observed before death. Consequently, it is argued, the appropriate measure is (and can only be) the value of the risk of death. In his original statement of this position, Misham (1971) concludes that, despite its practical difficulties, willingness to pay is the preferred measurement technique. The justification of this draws upon the earlier dictum that 'there is more to be said for rough estimates of the precise concept than precise estimates of economically irrelevant concepts' (Misham, 1971:705). Misham's statement reveals a surprising but widespread misunderstanding of the role of social values in economic evaluation. It may be true that willingness to pay is the usual basis for evaluation in economics and it may be that it is generally acceptable in the sense that it captures widely-held values in a wide variety of contexts – buying cars, breakfast cereal, and so on. It is not, however, the only possible basis and the relevant issue is whether or not it is appropriate in the health sector for the achievement of social objectives. That is, the values that govern the purchase of cars and breakfast cereals need not be the same as the values that govern the purchase of health care.

The problems associated with evaluating life may appear intractable, but, as we have already seen in Chapter 1, it is an inescapable fact that when resources are scarce and when there is the possibility of saving life – even at extraordinary cost – we cannot avoid putting a 'price' on life and we do this regularly. When decisions are made, implicitly or explicitly, not to devote resources to an activity which will ultimately result in life saving (for example, converting our electricity to a lower, safer voltage or increasing our health budget) we are implicitly or explicitly comparing the value of life with the opportunity cost of the resources; that is, the improvement in the quality of life that could be obtained by spending the resources elsewhere. Similarly, we regularly allocate resources to activities which will result in the loss of life (for example, cars). Once again, a judgment is being made concerning the value of life and other benefits. Cost–benefit analysis has simply attempted to find a basis for making these judgments explicit and therefore consistent in different contexts.

Cost–Effectiveness Analysis

Because of the practical and ethical difficulties involved in reaching agreement about the monetary value of life, many non-economists have concluded that CBA is not a very useful technique for the allocation of resources (see, for example, Abel-Smith, 1985). Recognizing these problems, most economists have attempted to avoid the controversial issues by adopting one of the two remaining techniques: cost–effectiveness analysis or cost–utility analysis. Cost–effectiveness analysis (CEA) ranks alternative health programmes according to the cost of obtaining a unit of effectiveness. Typically, effectiveness is measured as outcome (for example, lives saved or life years gained) or, where the measurement of these is difficult, as an intermediate outcome (for example, number of positive diagnostic tests, number of people screened, successful operations). Programmes are given higher priority if the cost per unit of outcome is lower. Following this rule means that more patients can be provided with more health when the budget is finite. For example, Russell (1992) estimated that, with a budget of $US1 million, it was possible to save either 11 100 life years through influenza vaccination or 100 life years through pneumonia vaccination. With a budget of only $1 million, the first option ought to have priority, as suggested by CEA. The technique does not, however, indicate whether the budget of $1 million is appropriate or whether it should be increased to $2 million. This judgment must be made independently.[6]

While CEA has the advantage of not requiring benefits to be reduced to dollars, it is limited to the comparison of programmes where there is a common health outcome – a common unit of comparison. It cannot rank programmes with dissimilar outcomes. For example, if programme A can restore the sight of 20 patients and programme B can cure an acute respiratory problem for a similar number of patients, CEA can give little guidance on the appropriate priority for these options.

Cost–Utility Analysis and the QALY

The third form of economic evaluation, cost–utility analysis (CUA), emerged in response to a recognition that years of life are more or less valued according to the quality of the life. CUA employs the 'quality-adjusted life year' (QALY) as the unit of output. In its simplest form, this is a life year weighted by an index of the quality of life or utility (early analysts used the terms synonymously). For example, if the result of a life-saving intervention was that a patient spent 20 years in very poor health (as when dependent upon regular hospital dialysis), the QALY procedure would discount these years. If years on dialysis were judged to be worth only 57 per cent as much as years of normal health (as reported by Torrance, 1987), the 20 years of dialysis would be discounted to $20 \times 0.57 = 11.4$ QALYs and this would be the outcome included in CUA.[7] By tradition, the utility index is expressed as a fraction between zero (death) and unity (full health). Consequently, in the above example the utility index would be 0.57. Utility values less than zero have been observed: there are health states where people systematically indicate that they would rather be dead (for example, 'being confined to bed with severe pain') (ibid.).

Like CEA, CUA has the advantage of not needing to place a monetary value on life and, also like CEA, it does not indicate whether or not a budget is the right size. However, it shares the advantage of CBA over CEA of providing a unit of outcome which can be applied to a very wide range of (and, in principle, to all) health states, namely the QALY. While the technique is still comparatively young, a significant number of studies have been carried out and a number of QALY league tables have been produced (see Table 2.2). While such tables need to be treated with caution,[8] they suggest that some interventions will produce far more health from a limited budget than other interventions. From Table 2.2, an investment of £1 million in anti-smoking advice from GPs will yield 3704 QALYs; similar expenditure on hospital haemodialysis will yield only 45.

CUA begins with the insight that the quality and quantity of life are both important criteria for evaluating the benefits of a health care programme and that these must necessarily be combined implicitly or explicitly when costs and benefits are compared. Of course, the validity of the QALY approach depends upon the validity of the numerical value of the quality of life (QoL) discount factor – the utility index. A 10 per cent decrease in the index has the same numerical effect upon the number of QALYs as a 10 per cent decrease in the number of life years. For example, 10 years of life judged to be worth only 90 per cent as much as years of normal health ($10 \times 0.90 = 9$ QALYs) is equivalent to nine years of life in normal health ($9 \times 1 = 9$

Table 2.2 **Quality-adjusted life year (QALY) of competing therapies: some tentative estimates**

	Cost/QALY (£Aug. 1990)
Cholesterol testing and diet therapy only (all adults aged 40–69)	220
Neurosurgical intervention for head injury	240
GP advice to stop smoking	270
Neurosurgical intervention for subarachnoid haemorrhage	490
Anti-hypertensive therapy to prevent stroke (ages 45–64)	940
Pacemaker implantation	1 110
Hip replacement	1 140
Valve replacement for aortic stenosis	1 180
Cholesterol testing and treatment	1 480
Coronary artery bypass graft (CABG) (left main vessel disease, severe angina)	2 090
Kidney transplant	4 710
Breast cancer screening	5 780
Heart transplantation	7 840
Cholesterol testing and treatment (incrementally) of all adults 25–39 years	14 150
Home haemodialysis	17 260
CABG (one vessel disease, moderate angina)	18 830
Continuous ambulatory peritoneal dialysis	19 870
Hospital haemodialysis	21 970
Erythropoietin treatment for anaemia in dialysis patients (assuming a 10 per cent reduction in mortality)	54 380
Neurosurgical intervention for malignant intracranial tumours	107 780
Erythropoietin treatment for anaemia in dialysis (assuming no increase in survival)	126 290

Source: Maynard (1991).

QALYs). In this sense, the utility index is an exchange rate between the quality and quantity of life.

Including Quality of Life

It has, of course, always been recognized that QoL is an important part of health outcome, and the QALY – the economist's contribution – was not the first approach to its measurement. Medical research has for many years been using 'disease-specific' measurement instruments and there are now a very large number of these. In a recent review, Bowling (1995) examined 193 of them. Essentially, these disease-specific 'instruments' consist of a series of statements or items describing different facets of health states[9] which, in some cases, are grouped into different 'dimensions' of the disease.[10] Items may either require a simple yes/no response (pain is experienced or not) or they may provide different levels of response (there is no pain; pain is mild, moderate or intense), or the intensity of the problem may be rated on a 1–5 scale. Commonly, these instruments provide a score by adding up the number of positive responses or, in the case where items have multiple responses, giving a simple numerical value 1, 2, 3, ... to the different response levels which have been arranged so that higher scores correspond with worse (better) health states. Total scores are then obtained by adding up the numerical scores derived from the rank order of the statement. (For example, an individual who filled in a five-item instrument with the third, fourth, first, second and third response to each item, respectively, would receive a score of $3 + 4 + 1 + 2 + 3 = 13$.) Higher scores are then taken to indicate worse, overall health states with the numerical value indicating, in general terms, the severity of the state. Importantly, these scores are ordinal (they rank health states); they do not generally claim to have an interval property.[11] As a consequence of this, it is difficult to compare health improvement at the top and the bottom of the scale. For example, a five-point improvement does not mean the same when a person is comparatively healthy and when they are comparatively ill, as a change of five points does not have the same meaning along the scale.

In addition to the plethora of disease-specific instruments, there are a smaller number of 'generic instruments' designed to measure a wide range of health states associated with a variety of diseases. Breadth of scope is gained at the expense of sensitivity and, consequently, researchers often employ generic and disease-specific instruments simultaneously. Brooks (1995) lists eight such generic instruments, the most well known being the 'Sickness Impact Profile' (136 items), 'The Nottingham Health Profile' (45 items) and the 'SF36' (36 items). The latter, which is now the most widely used generic instrument, groups its items into eight dimensions: physical functioning, social functioning, vitality, bodily pains, general mental health, general health perceptions, role limitation physical and role limitation emotional.

While these instruments generally produce numerical scores for each of their dimensions, there has been resistance to the combination of dimensions into a single QoL score. The common argument is that items within a dimension can be combined as they are measuring the same concept, such as pain. But dimensions cannot be sensibly combined; the attributes are too heterogeneous. For example, it may be claimed that self-care and pain are so dissimilar that their combination into a single index makes no sense.

The argument is persuasive and has commonly been used against QALYs. It is also wrong. It is commonplace to compare and implicitly to quantify the value of totally different items. When a person in a shop is faced with multiple products to buy, a comparison must often be made between quite dissimilar attributes. Different items are combined into a single index when the GDP is calculated, even though the products vary from theatre tickets to vegetables to ingots of steel. Comparison is possible in the first case because it is the *values* of the products that are compared, and in the case of the GDP it is the *values* of the products that are combined. The products per se are not combined. Similarly, the values of dissimilar health states as measured by people's preferences can, in principle, be compared or combined if the measurement is carried out properly. The difficulty encountered by the generic instruments is that the simple scoring methods (for example, adding up the number of 'yes' responses) do not adequately measure people's preferences; it is because of the scoring methods that dimensions cannot sensibly be combined.

Measuring QALYs

The distinctive feature of the QALY is that it measures people's preferences for (quite dissimilar) health states and it does so in a way that, in principle, should produce an index number with an interval property. There are two distinct steps. First, the health state to be measured must be observed and described. Second, a numerical preference or utility score must be attached to the description. In practice, these tasks have been approached in two quite separate ways. First, generic multi-attribute utility (MAU) instruments have been used. Initially, these are constructed in the same way as the generic profile instruments discussed above. A series of multi-response items are constructed. These represent the 'descriptive system' which should be capable of representing the health state being evaluated. The average utility (strength of preference) for each health state is then obtained during a series of interviews in which health state descriptions are converted into numerical values using one of the 'scaling techniques' described below. For example, relative to full health, which has a numerical value of unity (1), patients with diabetes may have a utility value of 0.85. In all but the simplest instruments, the number of possible health states defined by the instrument is far too great for direct observation of the utility value of every state and, as a consequence, a limited number of utility values are observed and the remainder of the health states are estimated from these.[12]

Researchers may use an MAU instrument either by circulating the descriptive system to patients before and after a medical intervention or, more generally and less accurately, by having an expert (such as a doctor) fill in the (believed) health state of typical patients before and after an intervention. In either case, the researcher may subsequently estimate the utility score of the health states from the values obtained from the initial interviews.

Five MAU instruments have been commonly used, another three are under construction,[13] and a simple generic utility instrument has been used by the World Bank to measure the burden of disease with a QALY-based measure (the DALY).[14] The earliest American instrument, the Quality of Well Being (QWB) was used in the famous – or infamous – Oregon Experiment in which all Medicaid procedures were subject to cost–utility analysis. The first UK instrument constructed by Rosser and Kind employed only two dimensions (distress and disability) and, including death, defined only 29 health states. Because of its simplicity, it is the only instrument for which all health states were directly evaluated. However, its simplicity and insensitivity have attracted widespread criticism: many UK commentators have equated the QALY method with the use of this instrument and criticized the entire approach on the basis of this instrument's shortcomings. Other MAU instruments include the Canadian Health Utility Index (HUI) Mark I and II, the Finnish 15D and the European EuroQoL. In 1997, three other instruments are nearing completion: the Australian AQoL, the HUI Mark III and the World Health Organization's WHOQoL. The Organization for Economic Cooperation and Development (OECD) is also considering the construction of such an instrument.

Once a generic MAU instrument has been constructed, it permits the fairly rapid calculation of utility scores, but it has limitations. Its descriptive system is necessarily limited. Instruments may describe health states with greater or lesser accuracy and, generally, the smaller the instrument the less sensitive it will be to differences in health states. For example, the simple Rosser–Kind instrument cannot distinguish the many sources of distress, such as distress arising from the social context of the problem and distress arising from the medical context of the problem, even though both may be of considerable importance for patient well-being. None of the MAU instruments constructed so far takes account of temporal aspects of people's preferences: a health state such as paraplegia may be intolerable in the short term but less so in the longer term as the result of 'adaptation'. Conversely, a problem such as pain may not be too troublesome in the short run but become increasing unacceptable in the long run because of 'saturation'.

The second, slower, approach to obtaining QALY values overcomes this limitation. With this approach, the health state is not described using a generic instrument; rather, a health state-specific 'scenario' or 'vignette' is constructed and then 'scaled'; that is, a numerical value is attached to the scenario. More specifically, individuals in the health state to be measured are interviewed using the techniques of qualitative research to determine which aspects of the health state are of importance to them. Any concern is of relevance. For some, the important aspect of the health state may be the effect upon mobility. For others, it may be the detrimental impact upon social and personal relationships.[15] The health state, as described by patients, is summarized in a written scenario and presented to individuals in the second stage designed to convert the health state into a utility number.

At this point the same issue arises as with the generic approach – namely, which scaling technique should be used to convert the description into a utility index? As previously noted, the numerical value attached to a health state represents the exchange rate between the quantity and quality of life. Five techniques have been used to establish this exchange rate. The first two, used by the early US and UK instruments, were the rating scale (QWB) and magnitude estimation (Rosser–Kind). Both techniques have a long history in psychometrics, where controversy still exists over which is the more appropriate in particular contexts.

A typical rating scale consists of a line on a page with clearly defined end points. The most preferred health state is placed at one end of the line and the least preferred at the other end. The remaining health states are placed on the line between these two in order of their preference, and in such a way that the intervals between the placements correspond to the differences in preference as perceived by the subjects. With magnitude estimation, subjects are asked to state how many times worse is state 2 than the reference state 1; how many times worse is state 3, state 4, and so forth, than the reference state. The essential difference from the rating scale – and the difference which appears responsible for the differing values – is the open-endedness of the possible values; there is no upper limit to the value that may be given.

More recently, economists have argued against the use of these psychometric techniques on the ground that there is no clear meaning associated with the numbers (see Nord, 1990; Richardson, 1994). Three alternatives have been suggested: the standard gamble (SG), the time trade-off (TTO) and the person trade-off (PTO). Each involves subjects directly comparing the quality of life with death.

With the standard gamble, the subject is offered two alternatives. Alternative 1 is a treatment with two possible outcomes. With probability p the patient is returned to normal health and lives for the remainder of his life; with probability (1–p) the patient dies immediately. Alternative 2 is the certainty of living in the health state being evaluated for the remainder of the subject's life. Probability p is varied until the respondent is indifferent between the two alternatives. The probability at this point is taken to represent the utility index.[16] For some economists, the standard gamble is the gold standard (Torrance, 1986) and it was for this reason that it was selected to scale the Canadian HUI Mark II. However, its status as a gold standard depends upon the validity of the von Neumann–Morgenstern axioms,[17] which have been subject to serious theoretical and empirical criticism. For this reason, the standard gamble can only be considered one of several competing techniques.

With the time trade-off, the subject is offered two alternatives: alternative 1 (the health state, S, to be evaluated) for time t (often the life expectancy of the individual with the chronic condition) followed by death; and alternative 2, which is healthy life for a lesser period of time x followed by death. Time x is varied until the respondent is indifferent between the two alternatives, at which point the utility value for state S is given by $U = x/t$. For some, this is the preferred technique as it most directly exposes the subject to the trade-off between life and quality of life (Mooney and Olsen, 1994; Richardson, 1994). Others have argued for its use primarily for practical reasons, such as its simplicity and the statistical properties of survey results (Dolan *et al.*, 1996a).

Finally, with the person trade-off technique, respondents are asked to compare two options, both involving health improvement for a different number of people. The number of people in one option is varied until the two options are considered to be equally desirable. The relative utility of the health improvements can then be inferred from the size of the two groups. For example, preventing the death ($U = 0$) of 10 people who will then remain in a poor health state S (Utility U_s), may be valued as highly as saving the life of x people and restoring them to full health (Utility 1.0). In this case $10 (U_s - 0) = x \cdot (1-0)$ or $U_s = x/10$. Recently, Nord (1996) has argued for the use of this technique.

As the von Neumann–Morgenstern axioms are problematic, none of these techniques can be considered a gold standard and each is confounded by a potentially irrelevant consideration. The standard gamble involves an artificial risk (instant death) which may be dissimilar to the real-world choice. The time trade-off involves two periods of time and the rate at which future time is 'discounted' is still open to debate. The person trade-off involves an impersonal trade-off between two groups and also brings equity into the judgment. Nord argues that this is a desirable attribute as populations are concerned with equity, but in the PTO the trade-off between the numbers of patients treated is part of the technique and not necessarily a description of the real alternatives facing policy makers.

In practice, all of the techniques described here have been used to produce QALYs. Some of the results from these studies are reported in Table 2.3.

Table 2.3   Some utilities for health states

Health state	Utility
Healthy (reference state)	1.00
Life with menopausal symptoms (judgment)	0.99
Side-effects of hypertension treatment (judgment)	0.95–0.99
Mild angina (judgment)	0.90
Kidney transplant (TTO, patients with transplants)	0.84
Moderate angina (judgment)	0.70
Some physical and role limitation with occasional pain (TTO)	0.67
Hospital dialysis (TTO, dialysis patients)	0.57
Hospital dialysis (TTO, general public)	0.56
Severe angina (judgment)	0.50
Anxious/depressed and lonely much of the time (TTO)	0.45
Being blind or deaf or dumb (TTO)	0.39
Hospital confinement (TTO)	0.33
Mechanical aids to walk and learning disabled (TTO)	0.31
Dead (reference state)	0.00
Quadriplegic, blind and depressed (TTO)	<0.00
Confined to bed with severe pain (ratio)	<0.00
Unconscious (ratio)	<0.00

Notes: TTO: time trade-off; judgment: no formal scaling technique used; ratio: magnitude estimation.

Source: Torrance (1987).

Types of QALYs

In 1989, Mehrez and Gafni proposed that conventional QALYs should be replaced by the Healthy Year Equivalent (HYE) (Mehrez and Gafni, 1989). The suggestion has led to a lengthy debate.[18] The conventional QALY is calculated, as shown earlier, by multiplying the number of years in a health state by the utility index which applies to *one year* in that health state. By contrast, the HYE is based upon a scenario which extends for a stated length of time that corresponds to the actual health state being considered. The standard gamble technique is used to derive an equivalent number of healthy years to the time in the health state.[19]

The HYE is, in effect, a particular type of QALY, whose distinguishing characteristic it retains, namely that it combines the quality and quantity of life. Its distinctive features are that it expressly incorporates a realistic time span in the health state scenario and that it employs the standard gamble. This second characteristic is considered important in order to link the evaluation task to mainstream economic theory via the assumption of the von Neumann–Morgenstern axioms. As previously noted, however, the theoretical and empirical evidence does not support the superiority of this approach. On the other hand, incorporating a more realistic time frame is undoubtedly an improvement upon a technique which assumes that a point-in-time or a one-year utility value will apply to all subsequent years. But debate has focused on the issue of whether or not in this respect the HYE is different from the TTO-based QALY when the TTO technique is applied to the same time period as the HYE. The consensus in the literature is that the two techniques are, in fact, the same, except for the effect upon utility values of risk per se in the standard gamble-based HYE.

In sum, the incorporation of a realistic time frame into QALY calculations clearly improves descriptive accuracy but increases the amount of QALY research required. To adopt the HYE, a separate survey is required not only for every health state but for every period of time. There is clearly a trade-off between validity and feasibility.

The extension suggested by Mehrez and Gafni is only one of many extensions which could be made to increase the validity of the QALY. The HYE envisages a *single* health state with a defined realistic duration. However, health states often change during the progression of a disease and a further improvement would be to describe the entire multi-health state scenario (until death) to patients and to allow its simultaneous evaluation. This was done in the case of breast cancer by Richardson *et al.* (1996). The two chief conclusions of this study were that the single evaluation gave different results from the summation of the (three) constituent health states and, second, that patients had extreme difficulty absorbing and appreciating the multi-stage health scenario. Once again there is a trade-off between conceptual accuracy and feasibility.

A further possible extension of the simple QALY rests upon the distinction between anticipated and realized health states. If we lived in a libertarian world in which all decisions were driven by individual consumers of health care, decisions would be made by (competent) consumers before treatment was undertaken and the factors affecting the strength of preference for various health interventions would include risk, fear and, potentially, a range of other factors associated with anticipation. In the prevailing tradition of economists – 'welfarism' – all of these factors should be included in the QALY calculation. By contrast, the conventional QALY or HYE calculation follows more closely the older 'material welfare' tradition of economists in excluding some subjective, anticipated variables and focusing upon the realized health state which can be predicted with confidence for large groups by statistical means.

Two studies are of interest here. In the first, Cook *et al.* (1994) calculated QALY values based upon the actual number of life years lost because of gallstone surgery, and the QALY values obtained when actual years lost were replaced by a scenario describing the risk of death. The number of anticipated QALYs derived in this second calculation was significantly lower than the number of actual QALYs based upon the first method. Second, Smith (1996) examined the preferences of a group of patients with colon cancer and compared their actual behaviour with behaviour predicted by QALY calculations. The latter approach, applied to each individual, suggested that patients would not seek adjunct chemotherapy to accompany surgery: the adverse quality-of-life effects more than offset the value of additional life years. Despite this, virtually all of the small group of patients interviewed selected chemotherapy. Their explanation, when challenged with the apparent inconsistency in their stated preferences and behaviour, was that they anticipated that, if cancer recurred, they would regret their failure to undergo chemotherapy. As predicted by 'regret theory', anticipated regret in this case was sufficient to reverse the choice that would have been made on the basis of anticipated medical outcome alone. The sample in this study was very small and the importance of regret as a motive more generally is unknown.

In the tradition of welfarist economics, both the conventional QALY and HYE incorporate an individualistic, self-interested perspective. Both are based upon interviews in which respondents are asked to consider how they personally feel about various trade-offs between quantity and quality of life. A further modification to the procedure would occur if it were believed, for ethical reasons, that another perspective should be adopted. As we have seen, the PTO asks respondents to assume the perspective of an impersonal planner and to trade off the options for other individuals. Instruments also exist which modify the PTO by asking individuals to trade off two different groups (as with the PTO) but in the knowledge that they may be a member of one of these groups. In effect, they judge from behind a 'veil of ignorance' (see p. 13). It is also possible to obtain an impersonal perspective while avoiding the distributional implications of the PTO by asking people to trade off duration of life against quality of life (as with the TTO) on behalf of another individual. While there has been little discussion of these perspectives, it is known that they will produce different QALY values (Richardson and Nord, 1997).

Whose Preferences?

Clearly, whichever QALY technique is employed, its acceptability depends upon both its technical acceptability – its ability to measure reliably what it purports to measure – and its ethical foundations. This is generally true of any basis for evaluating medical outcome and is not unique to the QALY approach. However, the measurement of QALYs involves a number of technical issues that are specific to the technique. Many of these are reviewed elsewhere (see, especially, Froberg and Kane, 1989; Loomes and McKenzie, 1989; Richardson, 1991).

One broad category of problems involves measurement. Do health state descriptions accurately reflect true health states? Do different scaling techniques (the TTO, for example) give the same utility values? Are the utility values reliable (do retests produce the same results)? Does the utility value vary with the duration of the health state? Does utility vary by socioeconomic status? The second broad category of questions arises from the survey methods adopted. Who should be interviewed? Are patients' responses the same as those of non-patients? Do utilities depend upon the social context of the health state? Will stated utilities vary with the framing of questions and the reference points used in measurement instruments?

We look briefly here at the question of whose preferences should be sought in determining the undesirability of various health states. Of course, this would not be a problem if it could be shown that no major differences exist among alternative groups of raters. In this connection it is important to note that subjects are not asked to assess health care programmes (breast cancer screening programmes, transplant surgery programmes, intensive care units) about which non-experts can be expected to know very little. Rather, they are asked to evaluate various generic states of health, such as being constantly tired, or being unable to dress or bathe without assistance, or being confined to a wheelchair. Most people have at least some experience of conditions like these, or can imagine them without too much difficulty, though really imagining what it would be like to be blind or senile may present problems to those who have not experienced the condition, or had close contact with someone who has.

At present, the evidence is somewhat equivocal concerning whether major differences exist among alternative groups of raters. Froberg and Kane (1989:585) find little compelling evidence of differences due to demographic variables such as race, nationality, marital status, political persuasion or religion, but cite some evidence that medical knowledge of an illness may influence a person's judgments (cf. Brooks, 1991:42). Similarly, personal experience of an illness or disability may have some impact upon a person's assessment of its disutility. Sackett and Torrance (1978) suggest that age differences may also be relevant, but several other studies find little evidence of age-based variation in the assessment of health states (Rosser and Kind, 1978). As Froberg and Kane observe (1989:586), 'because some of the studies contain small numbers of subjects, and many showed a high degree of variability in the distribution of preferences, the results currently available may obscure meaningful differences among groups'. In this situation, it is important to be mindful of how the construction of health state indexes could be affected by the choice of subjects.

Patients

One solution to the problem of who should be interviewed is to seek the views of those who have experienced the particular health state in question, or who are close to someone who has experienced the condition. This approach is often defended on the ground that those who have had first-hand experience of a health state, or are close to someone who has, are better placed to judge how distressing or disabling it is. If we are seeking the utilities that people actually experience in various health states, the utilities of patients should be the gold standard. Who could better judge what it is like to be confined to a wheelchair than someone who has experienced it? But Torrance (1986:15–16) and Loomes and McKenzie (1989:305) note that patients who suffer from a particular disorder have an incentive to overstate the disutility of their condition relative to other groups in order to enhance the cost–utility of programmes aimed at the prevention and treatment of the disorder. This may be done unconsciously, or it may be the result of a deliberate attempt to ensure continued disability support or funding for research. Whatever the motive, it could bias the results in favour of a particular group.

Counterbalancing this, there is some evidence that patients in fact tend to give less negative ratings to the conditions from which they suffer (see Pearlman and Uhlmann, 1988; Najman and Levine, 1981; Kahneman and Varey, 1991). Those who suffer from medical conditions that affect their quality of life tend to modify their goals downward and accommodate themselves to their condition, whereas those who have not experienced a particular condition, or have not experienced it for a prolonged period of time, tend to overestimate its disutility. Thus, whereas QALYs based on quality-of-life measures obtained from those who have a condition may overestimate the benefit of a programme that leaves people in that condition, owing to the possibility of patients exaggerating its disutility for self-interested reasons, such QALYs may also *underestimate* the benefit of such a programme as a consequence of the tendency of patients to minimize its impact as a result of adjusting psychologically to their condition. The ultimate effects of these conflicting influences are unclear. It is a matter for further empirical research to determine whether and under what circumstances these two tendencies cancel each other out in the construction of health state indexes, or whether one predominates to the extent of distorting the final measures.

Yet another possibility, which partially avoids this problem, is to question potential patients only. For example, only women (who do not have the condition) would be surveyed on the distress and disability that might be associated with breast cancer, only men (who do not have the condition) would be surveyed on the distress and disability that might be associated with prostate cancer, and so on. These groups of potential patients could be specified even more narrowly; for example, only women above a certain age, who do not have the condition, could be surveyed on breast cancer. But this approach no less than the others requires justification. Again, there is an incentive for these particular groups to exaggerate the disutility associated with the particular conditions being assessed. Nor is there any general solution to the problem of how narrowly the group should be defined. And, of course, potential patients have not in the past, and may never in the future, experience the condition under consideration, which raises the question of whether they are therefore less well placed to pass judgment on the condition than actual patients.[20]

Health Professionals

A quite different approach, of course, is to seek the views of doctors, nurses and other health professionals. This approach is often defended on the ground that health professionals are more knowledgeable about the various health states in question, and have the widest experience of them through their contact with a range of patients. Also, because of their training and experience, there are fewer problems associated with describing the health states to doctors, nurses and so on; they are already familiar with the conditions being described. However, just as patients have an incentive to exaggerate the disutility of their own condition, so doctors and other health professionals have an incentive to exaggerate, possibly unwittingly, the disutility of those health states they specialize in treating.[21] Compounding this, any doctor whose judgment of a patient's quality of life was *higher* than the patient's own judgment might run the risk of being seen as insensitive to the patient's suffering. So there are obvious pressures on doctors to exaggerate the disutility of the conditions they treat. On the other hand, there may also be a tendency for health care professionals who are in day-to-day contact with patients suffering from a particular condition to underrate the disutility of that condition as a result of seeing patients successfully adjust themselves to it over time, just as patients themselves rate the severity of their conditions less as they become accustomed to them.[22]

Moreover, as Torrance points out (1986:16), there is an added danger of bias associated with ranking health states on the basis of information obtained from health professionals, 'due to the special age, sex and socio-economic status of health professionals'. It is debatable how great this danger is, for it is unclear to what extent age, sex and socioeconomic status influence assessments of health state utility, if at all. On the other hand, the possibility cannot be ruled out altogether. Until it is demonstrated that there are, or that there are not, differences in health state ratings between different age, sex and socioeconomic groups, it is not possible to determine how they might affect the construction of health state indexes for resource allocation purposes.

The General Public

Another approach is to survey a random sample of the general public. This approach minimizes the danger of bias due to age, sex, socioeconomic status, ethnic background, religious affiliation, and so on. It also minimizes the danger of bias due to exclusively concentrating on those who have personal experience of a disability or illness. Nevertheless, some groups are still in danger of being disenfranchised. As Loomes and McKenzie observe (1989:305): 'this raises obvious problems about the representation of those groups who may be unable to respond, such as those suffering from certain mental illnesses or handicaps, children, and perhaps those not yet born'. In brief, a random survey of the general public is still likely to let slip through its net the preferences of at least some groups whose interests are at stake.

On top of this, of course, there is the question of whether a person who has not experienced a health state, or at least been close to someone who has experienced it (such as a relative), can give a truly informed judgment: 'should we base our estimates of the quality of life of people suffering from angina, or those who are confined to a wheelchair after a road accident, or those who have had their larynxes removed, on the responses of a majority of people trying to *imagine* what life in those states would be like ...?' (ibid.). It might reasonably be thought that this is a particularly difficult problem if a man must imagine what it would be like to have a breast removed, or if a young person must imagine what it would be like to have Alzheimer's disease. On the other hand, as Loomes and McKenzie point out, using a representative cross-section of the population could be defended against this criticism on the ground that partial or imperfect knowledge is simply a fact of life (ibid.). Since it is the resources of society that are being used to fund the various health care programmes, the construction of health state measures should reflect the preferences of the general public, even if those preferences are imperfectly formed.

To lessen some of these problems, Mooney and Olsen (1994) suggest that a random sample of the population should be asked, not only for their values, but also what weight should be attached to their values. However, this does little to solve the problem. Why should 'a random sample of the population' rather than patients or physicians be asked what weight should be attached to their values? Why not ask patients what weights should be attached to the preferences of doctors and nurses? Why not ask doctors and nurses what weights should be attached to the preferences of the general public? This strategy does little to solve the original problem of whose preferences should be sought. It merely raises the question of whose views should be sought concerning whose views should be sought.

As already noted, another problem associated with obtaining health state utilities via questionnaires concerns the age and sex of those surveyed. For example, Carr-Hill (1989:474) notes how the age of those surveyed might influence their valuations of health states: 'a healthy person in a particular age group might rate a condition considerably less than 1.0 relative to *their own state now*, but as they grow older their expectations about health will have changed so that when the time comes, they will rate their new current health status as very close to the best possible (whilst recognising that they were previously more healthy)'. Add to this the likelihood that certain conditions – for example, lack of mobility – may be more or less burdensome depending on stage of life, and differences in health state valuation due to age become potentially significant. One possible response to this situation might be to construct different health state indexes for different age groups, but this leaves unsolved the problem of how to allocate resources *between* such groups. There would be no need for two sets of indexes unless they issued in different rankings for the allocation of resources. But then how are we to choose between them? Another possibility might be to allow these age-related differences to be averaged out in the construction of health state indexes, on the ground that any attempt to eliminate them involves a controversial moral judgment. But then the decision to average out such age-related differences is itself no less value-laden. It results in the young evaluating health states to which the elderly are susceptible, and vice versa, and this needs justification no less than the averaging out alternative.

Mixed Strategies

There is no reason in practice why a mixture of all of the above strategies could not be employed in an effort to determine the preferences of individuals for various health states – perhaps a representative cross-section of the population, together with a certain percentage of patients and experts added. But, of course, this is itself a substantive answer to the question of who should be interviewed. There would presumably be considerable controversy, for example, about what constitutes the appropriate ratios of doctors to patients, old to young, experts to non-experts, and so on. Moreover, this approach assumes that a panel constituted exclusively of physicians or exclusively of patients is not appropriate, and this assumption begs the question.

Stated and Revealed Preferences

Another important issue which needs further discussion is the problematic relationship between stated preferences and preferences revealed by behaviour. If behaviour predicted by QALYs does not correspond to actual behaviour then surely the technique is flawed. In the terminology of psychometrics, preference measurement should be 'valid'. It is, of course, difficult to compare stated and revealed preferences and very little evidence has emerged from the health sector. However the issue has been the subject of heated controversy in environmental economics. This has been fuelled by the use of a stated preference technique (contingent valuation) to assess environmental damages and, in particular, by the State of Alaska contracting with several researchers to undertake such studies to assess the losses and compensation due in the case of the oil spill from the supertanker *Exxon-Valdez* in Alaska, in 1989. Emerging from this debate there have been at least five comparisons between stated and revealed preferences which do not support the technique. This leads Diamond and Hausman (1994) to conclude that people do not have well-formed preferences for the environment and that their stated willingness to pay for environmental protection was an arbitrary value arising from the 'warm glow' generated by making a statement. By contrast, Haneman (1994) cites an additional five studies where stated and revealed preferences do correspond. These authors conclude that the failed studies were the result of poor methods and not the impossibility of the task.

To help resolve the issue, the US National and Oceanic and Atmospheric Administration (NOAA) established a panel chaired by two Nobel laureates in economics, Kenneth Arrow and Robert Solow. Their task was to review the theory and evidence concerning stated preference and, it was hoped, to resolve the controversy (at least to the satisfaction of economists!). Their report (NOAA Report, 1993) concluded that stated preferences were capable of reflecting true preferences but that this would only occur when a series of correct technical measures was adopted to ensure the reliability and validity of the results. These measures, listed in the report, are very similar to those that emerge from the QALY literature, and indicate that eliciting individual preferences is fraught with technical problems, but that these are not insurmountable.

It is important to note that any assessment of the quality of life will suffer from the problems outlined in this section, and not simply the QALY approach. They are problems inherent in the task of trying to gauge what utilities attach to various health states. So if quality of life is to be a factor in our allocation strategy, and we reject the idea of simply imposing judgments about quality of life on the community, or making arbitrary judgments, the problem of whose preferences should be sought, and how best to measure those preferences, cannot be avoided, and hence it is not a criticism of the QALY procedure per se.

Ethical Underpinning

The remaining precondition to the use of QALYs is that their ethical basis is acceptable. Two important principles underlie the measurement of QALYs. The first arises from the fact that 'benefits' are defined in terms of life extension and/or improvements in the quality of life. That is, QALYs are part of the consequentialist tradition in which benefits are defined in terms of ends and exclude processes or means. Only the consequences of an allocation decision are important – specifically, the number of QALYs gained. This implies that, at least in their simple form, other ethical principles are excluded from consideration. Benefits are not allocated on the basis of 'desert', 'merit', or 'need', for example.

The second principle is that the value of benefits is determined by people's preferences. The basis of the QALY method is therefore preference utilitarianism. The idea behind preference utilitarianism is that, when weighing up alternative courses of action, we should aim to maximize the satisfaction of preferences, taking into consideration everyone affected by a decision (see p. 10).[23] However, it is not clear whether this should be applied to anticipated outcomes and include such factors as anticipated regret or whether it should be limited to realized outcomes. Welfarism is based upon one ethical foundation and the material welfare tradition on another. In the libertarian model of 'welfarist' economics, revealed preferences and therefore anticipated preferences have overriding ethical significance. For example, if a person selected an option which minimized risk and the likelihood of regret, then, as a preference for this option had been revealed, it would be taken as producing greater utility. If the realized health states from this option were, in fact, poorer, this would have no moral significance. However, there is no consensus on the ethical basis for resource allocation in health. There is plentiful evidence that the object of social concern in the health sector is the realized health state of populations and not the maximization of even well-informed choice which, as noted earlier, may be influenced by risk attitude, anticipation, regret and so on, and not simply by the utility of the final health states. This would imply that 'free choice' might not fulfil social objectives even if QALYs were measuring health outcomes accurately. Recall the inconsistency noted by Smith between the stated and revealed preferences of patients with colon cancer (p. 31 above).

While utilitarianism is the natural basis of the QALY method, it would be wrong to identify maximizing QALYs with maximizing utility.[24] This is so because people have preferences for things other than improving their health. Two individuals may enjoy the same health-related quality of life and yet one may be happier than the other because they have a more interesting job or a more fulfilling marriage or live in a better neighbourhood. More of their other preferences are satisfied. Thus there is more to maximizing utility than maximizing QALYs, at least as they have been constructed to date. This is important because, if we expect QALYs to solve all of the problems connected with human welfare and misery, we should not be surprised if they fall short of the mark. However, this limitation must be considered in relation to the purpose of QALYs. QALYs were created to assist with economic evaluations of health programmes. To be a valid measure in this context they must be sensitive to *changes* that occur as a result of such programmes. There is no practical purpose in their measuring non-health-related quality of life if this will not change before and after the health programme has been implemented. This means, of course, that it would be misleading to regard the QALY value of a particular life as indicating the total utility that is being received.

There may even be theoretical advantages in not incorporating non-health benefits into QALYs. McTurk argues that QALYs can then be used as a benchmark, as something by reference to which we can assess trade-offs between health gains narrowly construed and other benefits flowing from the provision of health care, such as reassurance, or the knowledge that one's autonomy and dignity are being respected:

> Even if you wish to embrace a broader notion of benefits into your distributional concerns, in order to decide *which ones*, and to *what degree* they should be embraced, it will be useful to know the amount of health gain being sacrificed. The inevitable trade-offs between health gain, and the provision of non-health benefits in health care, and the fair distribution of both, are kept more explicit. (McTurk, 1994:30)

But there is a further and potentially more important reason why it may be wrong to regard the QALY as a complete measure of utility. (Henceforth we mean by 'QALY' the conventional QALY, which does not incorporate non-health-related preferences.) There is compelling evidence that people have a very strong preference for an equitable distribution of benefits or outcomes. This is at odds with simple QALY maximization and suggests that QALYs do not incorporate all of the factors that are relevant to equity and for which people might have a preference. Similarly, it is possible that people may have a preference for the treatment of more virtuous or more deprived individuals. This would not reflect a principle that necessarily conflicts with preference utilitarianism. Rather, it would indicate that QALYs measured in the way described above would be an incomplete measure of preferences.

However, it is important to note that QALYs are egalitarian in the sense that, if they are constructed properly, they reflect no preferences based on wealth, social standing, race, IQ or other morally irrelevant factors: 'the method is egalitarian within the health domain; that is, each individual's health is counted equally' (Torrance, 1986:17). Similarly, allocation on the basis of QALYs is egalitarian in the sense that programmes are prioritized according to their potential to produce QALYs – those programmes having the lowest cost/QALY ratio being ranked highest – without regard to the way the QALYs are distributed among particular individuals or groups. Unless there are overriding reasons for doing otherwise, everyone's

QALYs are counted equally, and no one stands in a privileged position in the calculations.

Utilitarianism, with its emphasis on maximizing benefits, is often contrasted with 'egalitarian' theories, which emphasize treating people equally. But this can be misleading, especially if treating people equally is identified with treating them justly, for justice can sometimes require treating people unequally. A teacher who punishes all of her students because some of them misbehave is treating some of them unjustly. Justice may require that individuals and groups be treated differently when this is appropriate. (Cf. Campbell, 1988:32–5; Vlastos, 1962:40–43.) Similarly, utilitarianism condones treating people differently when this will maximize utility, but all individuals are given equal consideration in the pursuit of this goal. This is captured in Bentham's dictum: 'Everybody to count for one, nobody for more than one.' Treating an increase in A's well-being as on a par with a similar increase in B's well-being is the utilitarian explication of that more fundamental notion of equality common to all plausible moral theories: each member of the community is entitled to be treated with equal concern and respect. So both utilitarianism and the QALY method have an egalitarian component built in.

Of course, it should not be thought that the QALY procedure commits us to the equal distribution of health care resources. On the contrary, the QALY method requires us to put resources where they will produce the most QALYs for each dollar of the health budget – and this might mean that some individuals and groups will get more resources than others, and some individuals and groups may get none. The QALY approach is 'egalitarian' in the sense that, if all else is equal, a QALY gain to one person is of the same value as a QALY gain to anyone else, not in the sense that it advocates the equal distribution of resources regardless of benefit.[25]

Although it is QALY gains to patients and potential patients that are principally at issue when health care programmes are being compared, other beneficiaries may also need to be taken into account. It has often been observed that some medical interventions may produce little gain for the patient but may significantly improve the quality of life of others indirectly. For example, the major benefit of moving a mentally handicapped child or a dependent elderly person out of the family and into institutional care may be felt by the family, friends and other principal carers of the patient. Loomes and McKenzie (1989:306) see this as a problem for cost–utility analysis: 'there is a danger that QALY measures based on valuations of individuals' own health states may neglect factors which policy makers concerned with a broader notion of social welfare might wish to take into account'. Similarly, Lockwood (1988:42) argues that 'a calculation based on QALYs leaves out of account the effects that deciding to treat this person rather than that might have on the lives of others'.

However, the QALY method incorporates no prohibitions against including QALY gains to family, friends, principal carers, or anyone else, in the calculation of the potential benefits of a health care programme. As Loomes and McKenzie rightly point out, a person who directly receives treatment is not necessarily the only, or even the chief, beneficiary. In trying to measure the benefits a programme will achieve, therefore, it would be misleading to focus exclusively on the well-being of individual patients without taking into account the potential gains and losses to their principal carers, especially if these gains or losses are significant.

Of course, it is impossible to calculate accurately the *total* benefits associated with a health care programme. They are too extensive, stretching far into the future, and potentially affecting large numbers of people in unknown ways. However, the fact that we cannot envisage the total immediate and distant, direct and indirect, consequences of a health care programme does not indicate an inadequacy of QALYs. As noted previously, QALY analysis is concerned with the evaluation of effects, and it is primarily the province of medical science to measure these effects in natural units. Imperfect measurement, however, is a practical human limitation. Health care allocation should be guided by careful consideration of the *expected* consequences of our decisions. As the QALY gains and losses become more remote, and less predictable, the effects of an allocation decision on those directly affected will become correspondingly more important. Nevertheless, the QALY method should not be interpreted so narrowly as to focus exclusively on the patient's own good: the final objective is QALY maximization (for each available dollar), not QALY maximization of individual patients only.

Because people have an interest in things other than increasing the quantity and quality of life (at least if the latter is restricted to health-related quality of life), and in particular because they have an interest in how QALYs are distributed, a number of economists have been exploring the possibility of deriving weights for different QALYs (Nord *et al.*, 1996; Williams, 1997). This would mean that some QALYs count for more than others. These explorations have not proceeded very far. At present there is no method for determining an appropriate weight to reflect the importance of distributional issues. This does not, of course, alter the relevance of the QALY or the case for basing the initial allocation of resources upon QALY analysis and subsequently modifying it in the light of equity factors that are relevant for utility but are not taken into account by the simple goal of QALY maximization. Nevertheless, these investigations into different weights for QALYs suggest that there may be circumstances in which the indications of a simple QALY calculation should be over-ridden. To illustrate this point, we turn in the next chapter to the problem of age discrimination.

Notes

1   We consider an interesting exception below: the person trade-off.
2   Of course, the values adopted by economists are not arbitrary. As far as possible they adopt the values that people reveal through their actions. For example, the value of leisure time is based upon the trade-off people adopt between leisure and work when this is possible: the value of leisure is equal to the value of (net) income that could have been earned.
3   Economic evaluation is usually based upon the assumption that relative prices (which signal costs and benefits) are fixed. Large-scale resource movements could invalidate this assumption and consequently macro-reallocation of resources could only occur iteratively with progressive adjustment for changing relative prices.
4   Using the technique of regression analysis, income is typically explained by all of the relevant characteristics of the job (education needed, years of experience and so on), including the risk of death. The coefficient on the risk variable is taken as indicating the compensation that was negotiated when the income was determined. For example, if risk R was measured as an annual probability of death, and the 'regression coefficient' on R was \$2 000 000, this would imply that, among the jobs analysed, an increase in the annual risk of death of 1 in 1000 was associated with an increased income of \$2000 after allowing for the other relevant characteristics of the jobs (income = ... \$2 000 000 R; implied compensation = change in income = \$2 000 000 $\times$ 1/1000 = \$2000).
5   The inference is based upon one of the three famous axioms of von Neumann–Morgenstern which underlie the so-called 'expected utility hypothesis' that is widely used in economics to analyse risk behaviour. The theoretical criticism of the axiom centres around the existence of a 'specific utility of risk or gambling': that is, the like or dislike of risk per se as distinct from the utilities of each of the possible outcomes of a gamble.
6   Of course, the technique can assist with this independent judgment. In the present example, if it is believed that 100 life years are worth more than \$1 million, the budget should be increased to include the purchase of pneumonia vaccinations.
7   If we wished to discount for future life years, a small additional adjustment to the calculation would be needed. (See Parsonage and Neuburger, 1992; Cairns, 1992.) It remains an open question, however, whether this should be done. Perhaps it is irrational for people to value their future lives less than their present lives. Or perhaps when people apparently judge their future lives to be of less value than their present lives they are really unconsciously importing into their deliberations the probability that they will not be alive in 20 years' time. But QALYs can be systematically adjusted for time discounting, if this is judged desirable.
8   For example, the effectiveness of any intervention is likely to decline as the simplest cases are treated first: marginal benefits and not average values are required. Furthermore, care must be taken to ensure that all of the studies have been carried out consistently. Of course, these qualifications apply to all comparative evaluations and not specifically to CUA.

9   For example, the Health Utility Index Mark II has seven items which are related to sensation, mobility, emotion, cognition, self-care, pain and fertility. Each item has multiple responses. For example, the four responses on the pain item vary from 'free of pain and discomfort' (level 1) to 'severe pain that prevents most activities' (level 5) (Feeny *et al.*, 1996).

10   The 15 items in the Australian Quality of Life (AQoL) Index are grouped into the five dimensions 'illness', 'independent living', 'social relationships', 'physical senses' and 'psychological well-being' (Hawthorne and Richardson, 1996).

11   An interval property means that changes in numerical scores correspond to changes in some objective magnitude. For example, on a scale measuring temperature, the difference between 10 and 12 degrees has the same effect upon the expansion of mercury as the difference between 20 and 22 degrees.

12   A number of instruments have used the techniques of multi-attribute modelling which impose a simple (additive or multiplicative) model upon the data which allow the inference of multi-attribute health states from the utility values of the individual attributes. In the case of the European Quality of Life (EuroQoL) instrument, a limited number of multi-attribute health states were measured and their values regressed against the values of the constituent attributes. The resulting regression equation allowed the calculation of all multi-attribute health state values.

13   References to these are as follows: Rosser–Kind (Kind and Rosser, 1988; Rosser, 1993), Quality of Well Being (Kaplan *et al.*, 1976; Kaplan and Bush, 1982; Kaplan *et al.*, 1993), Health Utility Index Mark I, II & III (HUI) (Torrance *et al.*, 1992; Boyle *et al.*, 1995; Torrance *et al.*, 1995; Feeny *et al.*, 1996), 15D (Sintonen, 1981; 1994; 1995; Sintonen and Pekurinen, 1993), the EuroQoL (EuroQoL Group, 1990; Brazier *et al.*, 1993; Gudex, 1994; Van Agt *et al.*, 1994) and Australian Quality of Life (AQoL) instrument (Hawthorne and Richardson, 1996).

14   The Disability Adjusted Life Year (DALY) is a person trade-off-based QALY weighted by an index of the value of life years at different ages (Murry and Lopez, 1996). We discuss the person trade-off below.

15   As an example, the following scenario was used by Richardson *et al.* (1996) in their analysis of mammography. 'Mrs B had a complete mastectomy for breast cancer 3 years ago. Her entire breast and some of the surrounding glands were removed. But the cancer has spread to her spine and right hip. She has constant pain in her lower back. She has injections most days to help this. She is unable to keep up her usual activities. She is almost always tired. Her husband has to do most of the housework and friends help out with meals. She thinks about dying a great deal. She discusses it with her husband and feels well supported. But her friends find it difficult to talk to her and keep telling her to be positive. She feels that her body has been mutilated. She is no longer interested in clothes or her appearance.'

16   If U is the utility of the health state, then at this point $U = p . U$ (full health) + $(1–p) U$ (death). Since U (full health) = 1 and U (death) = 0, $U = p$. Strictly, this arithmetic simplifies the true situation. To eliminate the probability from the equation and to reinterpret it as an index number, the von Neumann–Morgenstern assumption of linear transformation under risk is required. From this, the equation $U = p . U$ (full health), which still involves a probability, may be transformed by dividing each side by the fraction p. This produces $U/p = U$ (full health), an equation that has eliminated probability. From this $U = p$, where p is now a *fraction*, not a probability. If the assumption that preferences are invariant under linear transformation is untrue, the relationship between the probability p and the true index of utility is unclear.

17   See previous note.

18   See Loomes (1995), Johannesson (1995), Bleichrodt (1995), Culyer and Wagstaff (1995), Richardson (1994).

19   More specifically, the standard gamble technique is used to derive a utility index number (from the probability) which applies to the entire scenario. The index number is then converted into the number of healthy year equivalents through a second application of the standard gamble in which the probability value (of death) is fixed by the first-stage results and the number of healthy year equivalents is allowed to vary.

20   Kazan maintains that effective community consultation will be obtained, not by seeking the widest possible range of views, but through the development of methodologies that tap significant or representative viewpoints: 'Consultation is ... a process of obtaining diverse views, not necessarily everyone's views' (Kazan, 1990: 12). But how are significant or representative viewpoints to be identified?

21   For a discussion of self-serving biases, see Elster (1991) and Messick and Sentis (1983).

22   It is worth noting, however, that Pearlman and Uhlmann, as a result of an empirical study, concluded that 'physicians' ratings [of their patients' quality of life] were generally worse than and only weakly associated with the patients' ratings of quality of life in each chronic disease [studied]' (1988:M25).

23   According to classical utilitarianism, an action is right if it produces as much or more net happiness for all affected by it than any alternative action, and wrong if it does not. However, it is doubtful that happiness is the only valuable mental state, at least if happiness is interpreted too narrowly, as pleasure for example. Writers and composers often find their task frustrating and difficult, but nevertheless find the experience rewarding in some deeper way. We could, of course, expand the range of mental states deemed valuable, as Mill suggested (see Mill, 1973), but some in the utilitarian tradition have argued that this is a dead-end strategy. Thus Hare argues that, when weighing up alternative courses of action, we should aim to maximize preference satisfaction (considering everyone affected by our actions impartially) rather than happiness or pleasure.

24   In this connection it is also worth correcting a misleading statement by Wagstaff to the effect that QALYs are a measure of a person's health rather than the utility they derive from it (Wagstaff, 1991:21). This is not accurate. The QALY incorporates information about preferences for health states rather than health states themselves. It does not tell us about such medical conditions as arthritis, cancer and diabetes, but rather about the undesirability or 'disutility' of the consequences of such medical conditions: needing to use a wheelchair or walking stick, being in pain, having trouble dressing or bathing, and so. In this sense, the QALY is a measure of utility rather than health. However, it encapsulates only one component of utility, namely health-related quality of life.

25   Likewise, it would not be in keeping with the QALY approach to distribute one dose of a drug equally between two people if a full dose will save one life and a half dose will save no life at all (see Smart, 1987:293). If dividing the dose will result in the deaths of two people for no gain whatsoever, it is obviously not the course of action that will maximize QALYs.

3 Age Discrimination

Leaving aside the technical problems, the most common criticism of the QALY approach to health care allocation claims that it unfairly discriminates against some groups, such as the aged and the disabled. Although QALYs might be useful for deciding between different treatment options for individual patients, since what each patient wants from medical care is to maximize his or her own quality and quantity of life, QALY maximization fails as a way of dealing with the problem of distributive justice that arises when there is competition for resources.[1] We have already noted that QALYs are egalitarian in the sense that they incorporate no preferences based on race, gender, intelligence, and so on. And allocation on the basis of QALYs is egalitarian in the sense that, if the cost/QALY ratio of programme A is lower than the cost/QALY ratio of programme B, programme A should have priority (in the absence of compelling reasons for doing otherwise), irrespective of the way those QALYs are distributed throughout the population. It is irrelevant how the QALYs are distributed because everyone is considered equally; the aim is simply to maximize QALYs. But a number of critics have argued that QALY-based allocation is unfair, and results in distributions that are unjust, despite this egalitarianism. These critics argue that comparing the worth of various health care programmes in terms of QALYs, to the neglect of considering to whom they accrue, has implications that are incompatible with our considered moral judgments about fairness and justice.[2]

For example, Harris (1987), Rawles (1989), Hope *et al.* (1993) and Smith (1987), among others, have claimed that allocation on the basis of QALYs involves a comprehensive bias against the aged. Other things being equal, saving the lives of young people will always be productive of more QALYs than saving older people, since the young have more remaining life years than the aged. Following the cost-per-QALY prioritizing rule will thus result in a disproportionately large slice of the resource pie (people, facilities, equipment) being allocated to neonatal care, paediatrics and so on, and a paucity of resources being devoted to geriatric medicine and terminal care. Harris argues that such discrimination is no more justifiable than discrimination on the basis of race or gender (Harris, 1987:121).[3]

The accusation that the QALY procedure is 'ageist' is common. But it is unclear whether the fewer remaining life years of the aged as a group will in fact work to their advantage or disadvantage when it comes to allocating health care by QALYs. The guiding principle of QALY allocation is to seek the greatest number of QALYs possible for each available dollar of the health budget. Since the elderly as a group experience many more health problems than the young, they also stand to gain more in the form of QALYs from health care expenditure. Thus, while their fewer remaining life years are a disadvantage when it comes to calculating their QALY score, their greater susceptibility to illness and disease and thus greater potential to benefit from health care expenditure are an advantage. Whether the latter (their greater potential to benefit from health care expenditure) is sufficient to compensate for the former (their fewer remaining life years) is an empirical question to which the answer is unclear. But it cannot be assumed without further evidence that the aged as a group will be unfairly discriminated against, all things considered, when it comes to allocating health care on the basis of QALYs.

This will not satisfy some critics, however. They will insist that allocating health care on the basis of QALYs may still result in discrimination against individual elderly patients, regardless of whether the aged collectively receive more resources. For example, an elderly person needing coronary artery bypass surgery may do very badly on a QALY analysis in comparison with a younger person needing the same operation, precisely because they have fewer remaining life years. And this may be so even if the aged *overall* receive more resources. So, even if the QALY method allocates more resources to the aged collectively, once these resources are distributed over the greater number of elderly people needing them (because the elderly experience more health problems than the young), many individual elderly people will still get less than a younger person in comparable need precisely because they have fewer remaining life years – that is, because there are fewer QALYs to be gained. Critics of the QALY approach will argue that this is still discrimination on the basis of age, and is morally wrong.

The 'Fair Innings' Argument

It is common for those who think that resources should be placed where they will do the most good, which is the rationale of QALY maximization, to argue that it is right for younger people to get priority over older people when it comes to the allocation of resources, because the latter have already had a 'fair innings'. Clearly, whether this is a good defence of the QALY approach cannot be settled prior to an examination of the slippery notions of 'discrimination' and 'equality'. That these notions are problematic is shown by Daniels, who asks under what circumstances several people in an office building have equal access to a supply of coffee. Some considerations seem relatively unimportant: 'Should we worry about the fact that not all offices are equidistant from the pot? Some are thirty feet away, some only ten.... Should we worry that some colleagues use more calories in walking to the pot than others?' However, other considerations are clearly more weighty: 'If the lounge is open only to male colleagues, then female colleagues can complain they do not have equal access to the coffee. If the lounge is up a flight of stairs and there is no wheelchair ramp, then my paraplegic colleague may have a ground for claiming unequal access to the coffee' (Daniels, 1982:53).

An important lesson to be derived from this example is that it may be possible to secure equal access to a resource, in this case coffee, only by treating some people differently from others; sometimes steps may need to be taken to compensate for variations that confer an unfair advantage to begin with. For example, buying an urn for the private use of someone in a wheelchair, or spending money on installing wheelchair ramps, may be done in the service of securing *equality of access* to coffee-making facilities for everyone. So preferential treatment may sometimes be justifiable: it may redress an unfair advantage. In light of this, and acknowledging that there will be borderline cases, we may distinguish between a pejorative and a non-pejorative use of the word 'discriminatory', the former describing a practice having the effect of denying the equal consideration of interests, the latter having the effect of promoting (or at least not denying) the equal consideration of interests. To give a trivial example, if we say that someone has a 'discriminating' palate, implying that they are a good judge of wines, we are using the word in its non-pejorative sense: being 'discriminatory' in this sense is praiseworthy. Put otherwise, in many situations being *indiscriminate* is a moral failing.

Returning to health care allocation, a defender of QALY-based allocation might argue that discrimination against the aged is morally justifiable because it compensates for an unfair advantage. If it is 'discriminatory', it is so only in the non-pejorative sense. This position is defended by Lockwood (1988) and Kappel and Sandøe (1992), who argue that everyone deserves an equal opportunity to live a worthwhile life: to raise a family, achieve career success, develop their talents, or in general to satisfy whatever hopes and desires they may have. Favouring younger over older people in the allocation of health care is therefore morally defensible, because the aged have already had an opportunity to satisfy their desires or to realize their life plans. Younger patients deserve the same – they deserve 'equal access' to a rewarding life – and therefore should be favoured in the allocation of health care resources.

To be clear, we need to distinguish two different versions of this 'fair innings' argument. According to the first version, younger patients, no matter how much younger, should always get preference over older patients, no matter how much older, in the allocation of resources. According to the second version, younger patients should only get preference over older patients when the latter have crossed a threshold – that is, when they have lived long enough to have had a 'fair innings'. According to the first version of the argument, a three-year-old should get preference over a five-year-old, and a 59-year-old should get preference over a 61-year-old. But according to the second version, a difference of two years between children may not give one preference over the other, and a 59-year-old will only get preference over a 61-year-old if the cut-off point is, say, 60 years of age.[4]

The fair innings argument might initially seem promising as a way of defending QALY-based allocation against the criticism that it unfairly discriminates against the aged. However, neither version of the fair innings argument is really compatible with the QALY approach. It is an implication of both interpretations of this argument that, under certain circumstances, a younger patient may get preference over an older patient even if the greatest number of QALYs would be gained by treating the older patient. Consider a 40-year-old and a 20-year-old competing for life-saving resources. Suppose that, with treatment, the 40-year-old is expected to live in good health until he or she is 65, while with treatment the 20-year-old is expected to live in good health until he or she is 30. Imagine further that the cost of the treatments is the same. The first version of the fair innings argument dictates treating the 20-year-old, since:

> to treat the older person, letting the younger person die, would ... be inherently inequitable in terms of years of life lived: the younger person would get no more years than the relatively few he has already had, whereas the older person, who has already had more than the younger person, will get several more years. (Lockwood, 1988:50)[5]

Likewise, the second version of the fair innings argument dictates treating a younger person if an older person has crossed the threshold that qualifies him or her as having had a 'fair innings,' even if treating the older person will in fact produce more QALYs. If the older person has crossed the threshold of, say, 60 years, he or she will lose out to a younger patient, even if the younger patient stands to benefit less from treatment in terms of QALYs. Hence, again, the fair innings argument conflicts with QALY maximization as a decision rule, and thus cannot consistently be appealed to by a defender of the QALY approach to counter the criticism that it is biased against the aged.

Eliminating Ageism?

Of course, this only shows that allocation on the basis of QALYs is incompatible with the 'fair innings' argument. It does not show that the fair innings argument must be rejected. Perhaps, rather, we should reject the cost-per-QALY prioritizing rule and adopt in its place a strategy that will eliminate the effects of age bias altogether. One way of doing this would be to adjust the weights of QALYs according to age. For example, if the average lifespan is 100 years for both men and women and the aim is to eliminate age bias completely, we might automatically scale up by a factor of five the number of life years used in calculating the QALYs of an 80-year-old (so that the maximum QALY gain would be $20 \times 5 = 100$). In the same way, we could scale the life years of a 20-year-old by a factor of 1.25 (so that the maximum gain would be $80 \times 1.25 = 100$), and scale the life years of a newborn by a factor of 1.00, and so on. This would compensate for the fact that the 80-year-old has only 20 years to contribute towards any calculation of the QALYs he or she might gain from treatment, whereas the 20-year-old has 80, and the newborn 100.

However, this strategy is also unappealing to a defender of the QALY approach. Consider a series of treatments that will restore dying patients to their full life expectancy. If the number of life years used in the calculation of the QALYs of an 80-year-old is scaled up by a factor of 5, those of a 20-year-old by a factor of 1.25, and so on, health care will no longer be prioritized on the basis of quality-adjusted life years (QALYs), but on the basis of quality of life alone. This has the implication that an elderly person with only a few years to live, or perhaps only a few months, and a 20-year-old with 50 or 60 years to live, competing for limited resources, should be granted equal rights to those resources, if their quality of life is expected to be the same. This is so because, once the adjustments are made to eliminate completely the relevance of age, quality of life is the only remaining ground on which a choice can be made between them (assuming complete recovery to the full remaining years of life), and by hypothesis there is no difference in their quality of life.[6] This reveals, again, that the strategy of completely eliminating the relevance of remaining life years is incompatible with the QALY approach. The aim behind QALY-based allocation is to put resources where they will do the most good, and this is measured in terms of improvements in the quality and quantity of life. The QALY approach therefore cannot be defended against the charge of unfairly discriminating against the aged by eliminating the relevance of age altogether.

Maximizing QALYs and Maximizing Utility

A more promising way of defending QALY allocation against the criticism that it is biased against the aged requires a more detailed examination of the relationship between QALYs and utilitarianism. We have already noted (p. 39) that for a variety of reasons (employment status, marital status, nationality, personality type and so on) two individuals might enjoy the same health status and yet one might be happier or live a more fulfilling life than the other. This suggests that there is more to maximizing utility than maximizing QALYs. In particular, to maximize utility we might need to give greater weight to the QALYs of some people. Whereas giving greater weight to the QALYs of some individuals or groups than to others will not contribute to maximizing QALYs, it may contribute to the wider goal of maximizing utility. To give a simple example, if two individuals stand to gain the same number of QALYs from a medical procedure but one has many more dependants than the other, it would seem that more good will be achieved if the person with more dependants is given preference, if all else is equal. (Cf. Nielson, 1997: 215–216.)

So, just as the goal of maximizing QALYs must be distinguished from the goal of maximizing utility, so the principle of counting all QALYs equally must be distinguished from the principle of counting all utility gains equally. Maximizing the welfare of the community is the overriding goal, and treating all utility gains equally, regardless of who the particular beneficiary is, is the essence of utilitarian justice: 'Everybody to count for one, nobody for more than one.' The cost-per-QALY prioritizing rule is a means of achieving this in the health area, and the principle of treating QALYs equally may need to be compromised if doing so will increase social welfare – if it will maximize the satisfaction of people's preferences overall, including, but not restricted to, their preferences for health. This opens up a new possibility: if the principle of counting everyone's QALYs equally can be overridden in the interests of maximizing utility more generally, perhaps it is justifiable, in particular, to override the principle of treating QALYs equally to ensure that the elderly receive more resources than they would on a simple cost-per-QALY calculation (or, indeed, to ensure that they are given less). In other words, perhaps it is justifiable to give more (or less) weight to the fewer QALYs older people have remaining, if this will result in more good generally – if it will maximize people's preferences for a more equitable distribution of resources, for example.

Several studies, including the Australian survey we report in Chapter 6, reveal that people have a strong resistance to discrimination against the aged in the allocation of life-saving treatments. The reasoning behind this is not clear. Perhaps some people feel that it would adversely affect their enjoyment of life, even while young, if they faced the prospect of receiving less health care in old age than they would receive if they were younger. Perhaps some people are repelled by the thought of witnessing their loved ones enduring neglect under a policy of age discrimination, or anticipate feeling guilty at violating such traditional values as respect for the elderly and the duties of children to parents. Yet others may feel that discrimination against the aged is intrinsically wrong. Whatever the reasoning, if allocation on the basis of QALYs threatens to diminish social welfare, the QALYs of the aged can be given a greater weight to avoid this.[7]

What this shows is that it is possible to justify giving the QALYs of the elderly a greater value *if* it is thought that this will prevent a decrease in social welfare, but it is an open question whether allocation on the basis of unweighted QALYs will in fact have this effect. After all, a disproportionately large component of total health care expenditure at present goes to the aged, and in this sense they contribute disproportionately to the social burden of financing health care. Even if the aged are disadvantaged by the cost-per-QALY decision rule (with no special weightings) and even if this results in some community dissatisfaction, this may nevertheless be compensated for by the benefits gained by releasing resources for other uses. As Battin observes:

> The elderly now use nearly a third of all health care. Were these resources reassigned to the younger and middle-aged groups, the probability would be dramatically increased that all or virtually all these persons (except the worst-off newborns and those catastrophically injured or killed outright in accidents, homicide, or suicide) would not only reach a normal life span but reach it in reasonably good health. (Battin, 1987:326)

If the currently escalating health care costs of the elderly could be significantly reduced, there would be more available for ensuring that everyone enjoys a higher quality of life. And this, of course, would benefit many elderly patients as well. If less were spent on high-cost, life-extending technologies for the elderly, for example, there would be more resources available for ensuring that everyone can enjoy a higher quality of life. Of course, it would take some political will to ensure that any resources saved by denying special consideration for the elderly (that is, by counting their QALYs as being equal with everyone else's) are in fact redirected to patients who can benefit more from them, or are used for some even more valuable purpose.

This being said, if discriminating against the aged in the allocation of health care will decrease social welfare, the simple goal of maximizing QALYs can be modified. It is a case where QALY maximization should take a back seat to utility maximization – that is, where the QALYs of the aged should be given greater weight in the interests of promoting a greater benefit overall (reducing fear, resentment, and so on). So, although QALY analysis is a tool for evaluating the allocation of health care resources, it is flexible enough to take account of wider social concerns, and can be seen as part of the attempt to promote the general welfare of the community. Should it turn out that the elderly are disadvantaged by the QALY method, as a result of which the overall good of the community is compromised, their QALYs can be given a greater weight in relation to other groups. This shows, of course, that the QALY method is only one part of the attempt to improve the lives of people.

At this point, the criticism that allocation on the basis of QALYs discriminates unfairly against the aged begins to look less damaging. QALY-based allocation is egalitarian in the sense that each individual's health is counted equally. But this notion of justice is restricted to the health domain and is therefore subordinate to the wider principle of justice inherent in utilitarian ethics: everybody to count for one, nobody for more than one. This means that, if a pattern of distribution based on the cost-per-QALY prioritizing rule is considered unfair or unjust, it is possible to modify the weights of QALYs to compensate. So considerations of justice inform the QALY approach, ultimately, via its embedding within utilitarian ethics. The aged are therefore protected from any bias inherent in QALY allocation by the utilitarian ideal that everybody (including the aged) should count for one, and nobody (including the young) should count for more than one.

Of course, this leaves utilitarianism itself in need of justification. In fact, if we situate the QALY approach within utilitarian ethics, it becomes rather artificial to separate the two, and we need to defend them as a package. The shortcomings, but also the strengths, of the two reflect upon one another. If utilitarianism turns out to be a flawed moral theory, this will reflect badly upon the QALY approach; but likewise, if the QALY approach turns out to be a defensible theory of resource allocation, we will have one more reason (though not, of course, a conclusive reason) for thinking that utilitarianism is not a flawed moral theory. Much of what we have to say in defence of the QALY approach in the remainder of this book, therefore, will swing between considerations relevant to the QALY approach in particular and its utilitarian foundations. But in the next section we consider a well-known alternative to the QALY approach.

The Prudential Lifespan Approach

Norman Daniels defends a view of age rationing that has a 'fair innings' component built in, a view of age rationing which, therefore, presents a challenge to the QALY approach. But Daniels sees the problem of distribution between age groups as one of rational choice (a question of how to defer resources from one stage of our lives to another) rather than as an interpersonal moral problem. He urges a shift from thinking of infants, adolescents, the middle-aged, the elderly, and so on, as distinct groups of individuals competing for scarce health care resources, to thinking of the elderly as the same persons as the young at a later stage of their lives. The problem then is not to allocate resources justly among competing groups, but to allocate resources wisely throughout the duration of our lives: 'we must *replace* the problem of finding a just distribution between "us" and "them" – between age groups – with the problem of finding a prudent allocation of resources for each stage of our lives' (Daniels, 1988:18). This changes the moral problem of how to distribute resources between age groups into a problem of rational choice. How should we distribute resources in order to best serve our interests throughout the duration of our lives?

According to Daniels, before we can solve this problem of rational choice we need to become clear on the function of health care. Daniels argues that health care is important because it plays a role in achieving, maintaining and restoring 'normal species functioning'. These activities are important because without 'species-typical' levels of functioning we have limited access to the normal range of opportunities open to individuals in our society. The normal opportunity range is 'the array of "life-plans" reasonable persons are likely to construct for themselves' (Daniels, 1983:508), relative to a society.[8] But of course, the particular goals a reasonable person may choose from this opportunity range will differ according to their stage of life: for most people, raising children will not be a central task towards the end of life, nor will establishing a career. With this in mind,

Daniels introduces the notion of an 'age-relative opportunity range': this is the range of opportunities available at each stage of our lives. Health care is important, according to Daniels, because in curing and preventing disease it restores and maintains our access to the normal range of opportunities open to individuals in our society, at our stage of life.

This then has implications for rationing between age groups; that is, for rationing throughout the duration of our lives. Daniels suggests that, if we knew nothing about our future health care needs, our financial situation, what sort of family responsibilities we might have, and so on, it would be prudent to distribute resources in a way that protected our access to the normal opportunity range at each stage of our life. For example, we might choose to reserve high-cost, life-extending technologies for our earlier years, and thus increase our chances of living a normal lifespan. The expense forgone in thus restricting costly life-saving treatments to our earlier years could be put to use in providing more social support services for ourselves in old age. 'I might reason that such services could vastly improve the quality of my years in old age and that such an improvement is worth the increased risk of a slightly shortened old age' (ibid.:496). This is not age bias in any morally objectionable sense, Daniels insists, because it takes place *within* lives rather than between them.

The first and most obvious problem with this account is that it is unclear just what constitutes 'normal species functioning'. For example, in determining the 'normal' lifespan for a member of our species, should we look at the life expectancies of people living today, or perhaps those of people living in the last century, or those of people that might live in the next century? Do we consider the lifespans of people living in developed, industrialized societies, where stress is high, or in rural communities, where stress might be less but diet and sanitary conditions are of a lower standard? These questions show that what constitutes a 'normal' lifespan for a member of our species is vague and changeable. Similarly, if a young woman is infertile because of blocked fallopian tubes, we might reasonably say that surgery that can successfully eliminate the blockage will restore 'normal species functioning'. But does *post-menopausal* infertility qualify as a disease – as something which compromises 'normal species functioning'? If what constitues a 'normal' lifespan for a member of our species can be influenced by social conditions (level of technological development, knowledge of nutrition and sanitation, and so on) why should not the capacity for post-menopausal women to become pregnant, which is also dependent on our level of technological development, our knowledge of reproduction, and so on, be considered a part of 'normal species functioning'? Of course, pregnancy after menopause is statistically rare, even today, as is living to

100 years of age. But Daniels denies the relevance of this ('dental caries may be nearly universal but still be diseases') (1989:679). So if something can be common and a disease and uncommon and not a disease (such as perfect pitch), why cannot childbearing for post-menopausal women, or living to 100 years of age, be considered 'normal'? All of this is intended merely to make the point that what constitutes 'normal species functioning' – the linchpin of Daniels's account – is quite vague.[9]

Another problem is that, even if we concentrate on those procedures that restore 'normal species functioning', assuming that it is useful to consider this a discrete category of health care use, it is not clear how Daniels's account ranks different uses within this category. According to Daniels, it is more important to prevent or cure those diseases that most compromise our 'species-typical' levels of functioning (Daniels, 1981:159). But can we really say that curing deafness does more to restore 'normal species functioning' than curing epilepsy? This is not a question that can be answered by an appeal to quality of life considerations because, according to Daniels, health care allocation is not, or should not be, concerned with maximizing the quality and quantity of life. Rather, it is a matter of achieving, maintaining and restoring 'normal species functioning', and in this way securing 'fair equality of opportunity'. But on what basis can we say that curing deafness does more to restore 'normal species functioning' than curing epilepsy or high blood pressure, or any number of other conditions?

Another problem with Daniels's approach, which remains even if we set aside these worries about the vagueness of the notion of 'normal species functioning', is that it appears to leave some important uses of health care out of account. For example, let us grant that cosmetic surgery and non-therapeutic abortion are not aimed at achieving, restoring, or maintaining 'normal species functioning'. (If the distinction between those procedures that improve and those that do not improve 'normal species functioning' is relevant at all, something must fall into the latter category, and cosmetic surgery and non-therapeutic abortion seem obvious candidates.) But if this is so, these procedures would not rate on Daniels's account, even if they can significantly improve the quality of life of those who receive them (see Jecker, 1989:666–7). In other words, since it does not prioritize resources for such things as cosmetic surgery and non-therapeutic abortion, Daniels's account is not really a theory of health care allocation at all. At best it prioritizes health care resources for *diseases*, where diseases are defined as conditions that compromise 'normal species functioning'.

Daniels is aware of this, but does not see it as a defect of his account. He acknowledges that there may be *other* grounds, apart from meeting health care needs, for funding such procedures as cosmetic surgery and non-therapeutic abortions: 'Where we think that meeting a non-health care need with medical technology is of considerable moral importance, as I think it is in the case of publicly funded abortions for Medicaid patients, we should have other reasons available than merely saying that an unwanted pregnancy is a disease' (Daniels, 1989:679). But this raises the obvious question: should restoring 'normal species functioning' be a higher priority than using health care resources for these other purposes? It is implausible to think that it always is, for we might be able to achieve much more good by utilizing our resources in other ways. For example, providing contraceptives in an underdeveloped country could hardly be described as restoring 'normal species functioning' (on the contrary, it might be described as interfering with 'normal species functioning'), but it might do more good than providing cochlea implants, or some other sophisticated medical procedure. Why do less good than we could otherwise do with our resources simply because we have a prior commitment to restoring 'normal species functioning'?[10] On the other hand, if we answer no – if we say that it is not always better to use health care resources to restore 'normal species functioning' – we need some way of deciding when restoring 'normal species functioning' should take priority and when it should not. If there are 'other reasons' for performing plastic surgery or non-therapeutic abortions, when and why should these take priority over restoring 'normal species functioning'?

One plausible answer to this question is implicit in the QALY approach: health care resources should be used to achieve the greatest increases in the quality and quantity of life (given budgetary constraints). When this can be effected by restoring 'normal species functioning', this should be the goal. When it can be effected by using the resources for 'other needs', this should be the goal. But this solution is unavailable to Daniels because it threatens to make redundant the distinction on which he builds his account. If we should utilize resources to maximize increases in the quality and quantity of life, the distinction Daniels draws between meeting 'health care needs' (that is, those uses of resources that achieve, maintain or restore 'normal species functioning') and meeting 'other needs' is irrelevant. What is important is achieving the greatest increases in the quality and quantity of life, as the QALY approach maintains.

In summary, the QALY approach has the advantage over Daniels's account of not relying on the unhelpful distinction between allocations that improve and those that do not improve 'normal species functioning'. This distinction is unhelpful because it shifts the focus from the main game, which is improving the quality and quantity of life. Most importantly, this distinction, as a basis for resource allocation, threatens to result in wastage by favouring uses that contribute to the achievement, maintenance and restoration of 'normal species functioning', even when more good can be achieved by using them for other purposes. By contrast, the QALY approach concentrates on improvements in the quality and quantity of life, and provides a general theory of health care allocation; it is not restricted to those uses that restore 'normal species functioning'.[11]

Four Problems for the QALY Approach

A Slippery Slope

We have suggested, as a way of dealing with the criticism that the QALY approach is 'ageist', that it may be justifiable to give more (or less) weight to the fewer QALYs older people have remaining, if this will result in more good generally. But a policy of adjusting the weights of QALYs is an acknowledgment that QALY maximization is not the sole guiding principle of health care allocation, and can be overridden. The challenge then is to contain the effects of this concession. The following principle is clearly problematic: 'If programme A has the potential for producing more QALYs than programme B for the same cost, then programme A should have priority, except where the aged are concerned, for their QALYs should count for more.' The problem, of course, is this: if the cost-per-QALY prioritizing rule can be overridden to benefit the elderly, why can it not be overridden to benefit any number of other groups? Put otherwise, the strategy of adjusting QALYs for age confronts the QALY procedure with a dilemma. If the cost-per-QALY decision rule allows only one exemption, the elderly, there will always be a doubt that this exemption is justified: why should the elderly be special? On the other hand, if there are several exemptions – perhaps those with dependants should also be exempt, or those at the peak of their earning power, or people of some social standing, or those who reveal by their behaviour that they value their health – this forces us to ask what such exemptions have in common, and to reject the cost-per-QALY prioritizing rule in favour of a more comprehensive principle.

However, this is not really the problem it seems, if we take account of the relationship between QALYs and utilitarianism outlined above. The QALY method is only one component of the enterprise of promoting social welfare, and can be seen as subordinate to the overriding goal of maximizing expected utility. Viewed in this way, there *is* a general principle in light of which we can explain exemptions to the principle of QALY maximization (per unit cost) – in light of which we can explain why the QALYs of the aged or some other group should get a greater weighting – and that is the principle of *utility* maximization. Any theory of health care allocation must be subordinate to the wider goal of promoting the good of the community, a fact that becomes obvious when we reflect that diverting resources from education, transport, housing and so on may produce more QALYs within the health sector, but only at the cost of producing greater misery elsewhere. So adjusting the QALYs of the aged does not start us down a slippery slope to unbridled, ad hoc exemptions to QALY maximization. The only justifiable exemptions are those that serve the goal of utility maximization: promoting the welfare of the community generally.

Utility and Fairness

But it may still be thought that this defence of the QALY procedure does not really address what critics have in mind when they complain that QALYs discriminate against the aged. They are not complaining that QALY allocation will not produce overall social benefit; they are complaining that allocation on the basis of QALYs perpetrates some unfairness or injustice against the elderly. The point of the 'fair innings' argument was to counter this objection; to show that the QALY method is not incompatible with considerations of fairness. In rejecting the 'fair innings' argument, therefore, we appear to have rejected the one option that does at least directly tackle the criticism that allocation on the basis of QALYs is unfair.

The problem with this argument, however, is the underlying assumption that the QALY method incorporates no satisfactory account of fairness of its own. We have already noted that QALYs are egalitarian, in the sense that they incorporate no preferences about race, gender, social status, IQ and so on. And allocation on the basis of QALYs is fair in the sense that programmes are prioritized on the basis of their potential to produce improvements in the quality and quantity of life (within budgetary constraints), without regard to the way these benefits are distributed among particular individuals and groups. In this sense it is impartial. Unless there are overriding reasons for doing otherwise, such as preventing a general decrease in social welfare, everyone's QALYs are counted equally. Indeed, if an elderly person faced a greater potential QALY gain from treatment than a younger person, the elderly person would be a higher priority for treatment on a QALY-based assessment. Arguably, this account of fairness or justice is preferable to that underlying the 'fair innings' argument, because it is consonant with the principle of placing resources where they will achieve the most good, whereas the 'fair innings' argument would violate this principle in the interest of helping younger patients. The QALY approach therefore supports the simple but compelling idea that it can never be right to prefer a worse state of affairs to a better, whereas the 'fair innings' argument violates it. Indeed, if an older person faced a great gain and a younger person very little gain, the 'fair innings' argument might lead us to choose a much worse state of affairs in preference to a better one.

Rival Foundations

In defending QALY-based allocation against the charge that it is 'ageist', we have tied the QALY approach closely to utilitarianism and suggested that the strengths and weaknesses of utilitarianism have reverberations for the QALY approach, and vice versa. But QALY allocation and utilitarianism are not inseparable, and this may be thought to raise a problem. If we accept the close connection between the QALY approach and utilitarianism outlined above, we have a way of saving the cost-per-QALY prioritizing rule from the objection that it is age-biased: the strategy of maximizing QALYs per unit cost can be overridden if it comes into conflict with the wider goal of maximizing expected utility. But this may be thought to leave a significant gap in the argument. If the QALY method can be situated within utilitarianism, why can it not be situated within some other normative theory, say Kantian ethics? What is wrong with the following position: 'The strategy of QALY maximization (per unit cost) is fine up to a point, but if it conflicts with an absolute moral rule it must be overridden'?

Against this objection, however, it can be argued that the QALY method is more naturally conjoined with utilitarianism than with Kantian ethics or any other normative theory. Indeed, the QALY method (or cost–*utility* analysis) is a special form of utilitarianism; it is utilitarianism applied in the health area, where utility is identified with improvements in the quality and quantity of life. So tying the QALY method to utilitarianism is really 'tying' two consequentialist theories – one a special case of the other – whereas tying the QALY method to, say, Kantian ethics is tying a consequentialist theory to an ethic based on rules. The conjunction of utilitarianism and the QALY method can thus claim a coherence that the conjunction of any non-utilitarian theory and the QALY method cannot easily match.

As we have previously noted (p. 9), one formulation of Kant's categorical imperative tells us that we must always treat other people as ends, never simply as means. If Kant's theory provided the foundation for the QALY approach, therefore, it might be thought to place a defensible constraint on QALY maximization: QALY maximization is fine so long as it does not involve treating people merely as means. In contrast, it might be argued, people are indeed treated as expendable in a utilitarian calculation. The utilitarian constraint on QALY maximization, that the goal of maximizing QALYs can be overridden if it comes into conflict with the wider goal of maximizing utility, involves treating some people as means to promoting overall social welfare.

But this distinction between Kantian ethics and utilitarianism is misleading. What does it mean to treat other people as ends? On one plausible reading of this phrase, it means taking their interests or preferences (what they will for its own sake) as of equal importance to our own, if they are of the same strength. It means that we should not treat people differently simply because of who they are. But this is the principle underlying utilitarianism (and the QALY approach): everybody to count for one, nobody for more than one. Utilitarianism also, therefore, forbids our treating people merely as means in this sense. It requires us to pursue the goal of QALY maximization without favouritism: we should seek the greatest possible improvements in quality of life and quantity of life without deeming some people's interests of more importance simply because of who they are. If A receives the only available organ for transplant instead of B, because A can benefit more from it, this does not involve treating B as a means (given that all else is equal), because if the roles were reversed B would get the organ. Only when this commitment to impartiality is ignored does the danger of treating some people simply as means arise. So placing the QALY approach on a foundation of Kantian ethics is not required for avoiding the danger of treating some people simply as a means, in this sense. Placing it on a utilitarian foundation will also forbid our treating people merely as means. (Cf. Hare, 1993a:3–5; Nielson, 1997:216.)

Social Hijacking

Another problem with the QALY approach is raised by Rawls (1982) and Daniels (1981). Both note that some people have moderate tastes. Their expectations are such that they have a reasonable chance of being satisfied with their share of social goods. But other people have extravagant tastes. They will be unhappy with a comparable share of social goods.

> Then if we are interested in maximizing – or even equalizing – satisfaction, extravagants seem to have a greater claim on further distributions of social resources than moderates. But something seems clearly unjust if we deny the moderates equal claims on further distributions just because they have been modest in forming their tastes. (Daniels, 1981:161–2)

This might lead us to doubt whether we should allocate resources impartially so as to achieve the greatest increases in the quality and quantity of life, because this will expose the health care system to 'social hijacking' by persons with expensive tastes: some people will not be happy unless they have recourse to the most sophisticated and expensive treatments for the most minor conditions, whereas other people will be satisfied with less, and will therefore be disadvantaged because of their more moderate expectations.

Several considerations lessen the force of this objection. First, if we have to spend more on an 'extravagant' to achieve a similar benefit that spending less on a 'moderate', or several moderates, could achieve, this is not consonant with ranking treatments from the lowest *cost*/QALY ratio to the highest. The goal of maximizing QALYs requires that we use our limited resources efficiently, not squander them on extravagants.

Second, we have to distinguish clearly between, on the one hand, people who have a greater than usual capacity for enjoying life and, on the other, people who are greedy. It is questionable whether having a greater than usual capacity for enjoying life is really a character flaw, or something we should want to discourage. Imagine that two explorers with their supplies exhausted come across a flask of water in the desert. If one has a greater thirst than the other, it would seem only right that he or she should get the water in preference to the other person, or a greater share of it. Arguably, the thirstier individual has a greater claim on it, other things being equal, because that person will benefit from it more. Why should it be any different with a 'thirst for life'? If A has a greater capacity to benefit from social resources than B, it would seem only right to view A as having a greater entitlement to those resources, other things being equal. They are of more value to A.[12]

On the other hand, some people are simply greedy. They do not have a greater capacity for enjoying life, they simply demand more than others. Perhaps it is these people Rawls and Daniels have in mind when they speak of social hijacking by 'extravagants'. This is not really a problem for utilitarianism, however, for as Daniels acknowledges (1981:n 23), it is in everyone's interests in the long run to discourage greed and selfishness. Pandering to greed – indulging preferences that can only be fulfilled at excessive cost – will obviously not maximize welfare in the long run. So the utilitarian also will seek to avoid, rather than promote, social hijacking by extravagants.[13]

Provisionally, then, the QALY approach would appear not to be under threat from the criticism that it discriminates unfairly against the aged. At least, the threat is less serious than it might initially have seemed if the QALY method is properly understood. First, owing to the way they are constructed, QALYs carry no inherent bias against the aged; they reflect people's preferences for health states only. Second, the flexibility of the QALY approach means that the QALYs of some groups, including the aged, can in fact be weighted differently, if this is necessary to compensate for any unfair disadvantage that jeopardizes social welfare. Viewed in this way, the charge that allocating on the basis of QALYs is incompatible with respect for the aged loses much of its force.

Saving Lives versus Maximizing QALYs

In Chapter 2, we saw that the QALY represents a promising way of combining the quality and quantity of life into a single measure of health care outcome, so that those who have responsibility for funding health care can compare treatments and programmes in different areas. Cost–benefit analysis also allows the comparison of treatments and programmes in different areas, but only because it reduces all of the potential benefits of health care to monetary terms. However, a similar problem confronts both the QALY approach and CBA, for whereas CBA, by focusing exclusively on monetary gains and losses, neglects something of even greater concern, namely, improvements in the quality and quantity of life, so the QALY approach, by focusing exclusively on QALY gains and losses, neglects something of even greater concern, namely, people. Or so it has been argued. If the goal is to maximize QALYs per unit cost, some critics say, individuals are not being accorded the prime importance in our moral theory they deserve. Life years, whether quality-adjusted or not, are in some sense of secondary importance, people of prime importance.

One consequence of this emphasis on QALYs rather than people can be seen in another allocation problem raised by Jonathan Glover (1977:221) and discussed by John Harris (1985: ch. 5), among others. Suppose it costs $7000 to extend the lives of seven people for one year and $6000 to extend the life of one person for seven years, and we cannot do both. Assume also that without treatment the life expectancy of everyone concerned is zero, whereas with treatment all will enjoy good health until death. If we believe that resources ought to be allocated on the basis of QALYs, we should prefer the second alternative, since the anticipated QALY gain is the same but the second option is cheaper, indicating that this option gives better value for money, where value is measured in QALYs. But is this the right answer?[14]

Harris (1987:118) argues that it is not. If all those concerned *want* to go on living, if they all prefer continued life to immediate death, the second alternative is unacceptable: it has the effect of sacrificing six lives for one. Contrary to the QALY approach, Harris maintains, postponing the deaths of a greater number of people, even for a comparatively short time, should take priority over postponing the deaths of a smaller number of people for a longer time: 'each life counts for one and that is why more count for more' (ibid.:120). The problem with QALY-based allocation is that 'it establishes life units, in this case life-years, as the entities which have value and which are to be maximised. On this view it is not people who are valued, it is not people who are to be protected by the equality principle, but simply units of lifetime' (Harris, 1988:79).

By contrast, Harris holds that society should value the lives of its citizens and ensure that as few of them die prematurely as possible. If a person values their life and wants to go on living, they suffer a terrible injustice if that life is cut prematurely short, whether they have six months to live or six years. Thus, according to Harris, it is better to save the lives of seven people, if only for one year, than to save the life of one person for seven years, even if the former option is more expensive.

Note that a corresponding problem arises if the potential improvement is with respect to quality of life rather than life expectancy. Suppose it costs $7000 to increase the quality-of-life score of three people from 0.7 to 0.8 and $6000 to increase the quality-of-life score of one person from 0.7 to 1.00. In this case, also, a simple QALY calculation indicates that we should prefer the second alternative, if all else is equal, since the anticipated QALY gain is the same but the second option is cheaper, indicating better value for money. But according to Harris, it is wrong to confer all the benefit on one individual, if all those concerned *want* the envisaged improvement to their quality of life. A situation where a few are better off and many are worse off cannot be preferable to a situation where many are better off and a few are worse off, even if the cost per QALY for bringing about the former situation is less.

Harris himself raises an obvious objection to the idea that postponing the deaths of more people, for a comparatively short time, should take priority over postponing the deaths of fewer people for a longer period of time. Imagine that a choice must be made between extending the life of one person for seven years and extending the lives of thousands of people for seven hours or seven minutes. In this situation, Harris acknowledges, it is questionable that we should dissipate the potential benefits among huge numbers at the expense of securing a substantial benefit for one individual, if the aggregate number of life years expected to be gained is the same in both cases and the quality of life is expected to be the same for all concerned. 'Normally, we want to have our death postponed for as long as possible but where what's possible is the gaining of only very short periods of remission, hours or days, these may not be worth having' (Harris, 1987:120). In this situation, Harris acknowledges, it may be better to postpone the death of one person for seven years at the expense of (in effect) slightly hastening the deaths of several thousand, especially if the first option is cheaper.

Of course, this appears to be inconsistent with Harris's contention that society should principally value the lives of its citizens and ensure that as few of them die prematurely as possible. However, he tentatively suggests a way of dealing with this difficulty: perhaps 'we can discount small gains in time as below the level of discrimination' (Harris, 1985:97). If the period of time for which death is expected to be delayed for those in the larger group falls below the level of discrimination it should be deemed 'nugatory' and should not count when a period of time above the threshold can be secured for an individual or a smaller group. Although it is better to give resources to more people rather than fewer when the individuals concerned will gain years, it is less plausible when they will gain weeks or days, or perhaps only hours or minutes – that is, periods that fall below the threshold. In order to stop this slide down the slippery slope, Harris posits the idea of a *threshold of discrimination*.

The first point to note about this suggestion is the rather misleading use of the expression 'threshold of discrimination'. It suggests the value-free notion of time discrimination; for example, the ability of human beings to experience very brief periods of time or to distinguish between events that occur very rapidly in succession. But when we are considering whether 'days or hours' fall below the level of discrimination it cannot be time discrimination that is at issue, since the real threshold of time discrimination is well below a second. Rather, the suggestion is that there is a threshold by reference to which we can 'discriminate' between periods of time that are, and those that are not, *valuable to individuals who receive them*. The suggestion is the value-laden, rather than value-neutral, one that gains in time should be disregarded (considered 'nugatory') when they are 'not worth having'.[15]

The crucial question then is: just when is an extension of life worth having and when is it not worth having? In other words, exactly where is the threshold of discrimination? Harris suggests that it should be left up to individuals themselves to decide whether the postponement of their own death for a certain period of time is worthwhile: 'even brief remission can be valuable in enabling the individual to put her affairs in order, make farewells and so on, and this can be important. It is for the individual to decide whether the remission that she can be granted is worth having' (Harris, 1987:120–21). This is a laudable position to take when the question of limited resources is not an issue: when there is no competition for resources. Patients (in consultation with their physicians, families and so on) should decide whether they want life-prolonging treatment, when it is available, or whether they wish to forgo such treatment. To say this is to endorse voluntary euthanasia, and respect patient autonomy, rather than defend any particular position on how scarce resources should be allocated. But when more people want resources than are available – when there is competition for resources – this approach will not work. Allowing individuals to decide who among them should get life-prolonging treatment and who should not, in the context of competition for resources, will only lead to irresolvable stalemates: everyone will want to save or improve his or her own life. Similarly, it would not be practical to allow groups of patients to decide what resources should be devoted to the treatment of conditions to which they are prone, or from which they suffer, because, again, all groups would want as much as they could get.

The problem with Harris's suggestion of a threshold, then, is that he gives no information about where the threshold is, how it is to be drawn, or by whom. But this does not mean that the idea of a threshold itself should be rejected. If we accept that sometimes it may be best to help several individuals (when the period of time expected to be gained is significant) and sometimes best to help one individual (when the several individuals will only gain hours or minutes and the individual will gain years), it appears that the idea of a threshold has some plausibility. The problem is that Harris provides no principled way of determining where the threshold is. When is it best to help the smaller number and when is it best to help the larger number?

A possible solution to this problem is contained in our earlier analysis of the relationship between the QALY method and utilitarianism, though it is not one of which Harris would approve.[16] If we view QALY-based allocation as an application of utilitarianism in the health area, we can accept that the threshold is regulated by the ideal of *utility* maximization. Sometimes it might be best to postpone the death of one person, and sometimes it might be best to postpone the deaths of several, depending on the circumstances; that is, depending on which alternative will do the most good. As Harris acknowledges, if the larger group will only gain a few days or hours, whereas the single individual will gain several years, it will probably be best to postpone the death of the single individual: 'Normally, we want to have our death postponed for as long as possible but where what's possible is the gaining of only very short periods of remission, hours or days, these may not be worth having.' And it must be kept in mind that, if treating the single individual is also cheaper (in Harris's example it costs $6000 as opposed to $7000), there is another reason for preferring to help the single individual, for we can help others with the money we save.

Alternatively, there may be circumstances in which it is best to help the larger number of people, perhaps because of the threat posed to social welfare by doing otherwise. It is not unreasonable to think that resentment might build up in the community if a health policy required seven individuals to sacrifice a period of time as long as one year for the benefit of another individual, even if this other individual stood to gain seven years of good-quality life. Such resentment must be factored into a calculation of which option will do the most good, as must the anguish experienced by the families of the seven individuals.

The lesson to be derived from the problem Glover and Harris raise, then, is one with which we are now familiar: the directive to maximize QALYs, or to maximize QALYs for each dollar of cost, is too simple. Whether it is better to secure many QALYs for a few people or fewer QALYs for more people may differ according to the circumstances: in particular, on which option will do the most good. This means that the QALY method is only part of the total story of resource allocation. It is an important part, because it unquestionably enshrines two important goals of health care: improvements in quality of life and quantity of life. But circumstances may arise where we need to go beyond these criteria. Other factors bearing on social welfare may also need to be taken into account and, on occasions, these may be of paramount importance. As we have seen, QALYs encapsulate information about preferences for health states, but do not take into account other things that enhance, or detract from, an individual's life, or from social value. It is not surprising, then, that the QALY method alone does not give a definitive solution to the problem of whether we should secure many QALYs for a few people or fewer QALYs for many people. But to construe this as a criticism of the QALY method would be to have unreasonable expectations of it. QALYs do not, nor could they reasonably be expected to, encapsulate every possible factor that might carry some weight in the allocation of health care resources.

Notes

1   Even on the individual level, however, problems arise in the trade-off between quantity and quality of life. Those who hold a sanctity of life view, for example, may be reluctant to trade off any loss in length of life for any improvement in quality of life, and see it as morally wrong for others to do so. The application of the QALY procedure even on the individual level, therefore, is not uncontroversial.

2   It is worth keeping in mind that, even if the QALY approach does conflict with our particular moral judgments at certain points, it is a controversial matter just how serious a defect this is. Should we test our basic moral principles

against our particular moral judgments or test our particular moral judgments against our basic moral principles; or should we aim for some degree of 'reflective equilibrium', as Rawls suggests (see p. 8)? And if the latter, are particular moral judgments and basic moral principles the only factors that need to be brought into equilibrium ('narrow reflective equilibrium') or are background theories also relevant ('wide reflective equilibrium')? (Cf. Daniels, 1979a.)

3   Extending this criticism, Harris argues that QALY maximization dictates providing aid to a country whose citizens have a normal average age in preference to a country whose citizens have a high average age, even if the high average age of the latter country is a result of its young people being killed in a war, or lost to famine or some other natural disaster, because the lower the average age of (the citizens of) a country the higher the potential QALY gain (Harris, 1987:119).

4   Support for the second version of the fair innings argument might be sought in the views of Callahan on the goals of medicine (1987; 1991). Callahan argues that health care resources, even if they are relatively ample, should not be allocated with the aim of indefinitely extending the life of the elderly but only for the full achievement of a fitting lifespan. He maintains that there is a natural lifespan, which it is not desirable to strive to exceed.

5   Kappel and Sandøe hold the same view: 'If we give the liver to the older person, he will get another ten years on top of those 60 that he has already got. And he will end up with 70 life years. Whereas if we give the liver to the young person he will only end up with a total of thirty life years. To give the liver to the older person is like giving money to the rich rather than to the poor' (Kappel and Sandøe, 1992:314).

6   John Harris, in fact, defends precisely this position (for example, Harris, 1994). According to Harris, all lives are of equal value regardless of age (and, indeed, regardless of quality of life). We consider his arguments in Chapter 5.

7   As McTurk points out (1994:27), this separation of the question of what is good (maximizing QALYs) from the question of what is just (everybody to count for one, nobody for more than one) can be considered an advantage of the QALY approach: 'it can be considered a *benefit* of the QALY approach that if ... discrimination is found to be systematic, and the pattern of distribution is considered to be undesirable, it is possible to attach differential weights to QALYs according to the groups who will receive them, thereby redressing this problem. Such groups might include rural communities and those possessing certain social characteristics, as well as the elderly and the mentally handicapped. Equity weights allow considerations of fairness to be considered separately.'

8   'The range is thus relative to key features of the society – its stage of historical development, its level of material wealth and technological development, and even important cultural facts about it' (Daniels, 1983:508).

9   The same question might be asked of homosexuality. Is it a part of 'normal species functioning'? On this point, note Jecker: 'But even if species were fixed and unchanging and we had available to us a blueprint for the design of the human species, it is doubtful that it could serve as a quick reference guide for determining if some condition is a disease. ... we might not be willing to accept the suggestion that homosexuality is a disease, even if we were convinced that homosexual practices deviate from the characterization of sexual functioning stated in a design plan' (Jecker, 1989:669). Whether or not Jecker is right to doubt that homosexuality should be considered a disease even if we had a blueprint for the design of the human species, without such a blueprint it is certainly questionable whether homosexuality deviates from 'normal species functioning'.

10   Similarly, if two options both promise to restore 'normal species functioning', but one more than the other (given that this is a coherent notion), it is not clear that we should always prefer the first, for the second might achieve a greater overall improvement in the quality and quantity of life. Jecker sums up this problem succinctly (1989:672): 'It should come as no surprise that maintaining an organism's age-relative normal functioning can conflict with medical goals as well as meet them. After all, the goal of medicine is not merely to produce normal biological functioning, but to serve a patient's interests... . Serving a person's interests means not just serving a person *qua* biological organism, it means serving a person's overall well-being.'

11   It should also be noted that the prudential lifespan approach depends on a certain view of personal identity that might be questioned: namely, that we should think of the elderly as the *same persons* as the young at a later stage of their lives. Underlying this view is the assumption that personal identity is an all-or-nothing affair, and survives marked changes in character, beliefs, life-style, and so on. An alternative view has it that personal identity comes in degrees, corresponding to the degree of bodily and psychological connection between our earlier and later selves. If we take this view, the moral problem of distributing resources between groups of 'different' people, characterized by stage of life, re-emerges. For example, Daniels takes pains to point out that the qualified age rationing he supports is different from race discrimination or sex discrimination. In the latter cases, if we show preference for one group (for example, whites or males) we disadvantage a different group (for example, blacks or females). But if we show preference for the young we are not disadvantaging a *different* group – the old – for the young are just the old at a different stage of their lives. However, the disanalogy between racism and sexism, on the one hand, and Daniels's qualified age rationing, on the other, is weakened if we reject the view of personal identity underlying it; that is, if we reject the idea that the young are identical with the old in the sense that we are dealing with intra- rather than inter-personal moral issues. (For more on the connection between ethics and different views about personal identity, see Parfit, 1973.)

12   This does not mean that we should abandon those who have a diminished capacity to benefit from resources. For example, providing counselling and treatment for the clinically depressed can have very beneficial effects. If our goal is to achieve the greatest increases in the quality and quantity of life for our health care expenditure, it would be foolish to discriminate systematically against those who, at any point in time, have a diminished capacity to benefit from help. Sometimes the greatest good can be achieved precisely by helping these people.

13   Cohen makes a similar point (1993:13): 'To the extent that people are indeed responsible for their tastes, the relevant welfare deficits do not command the attention of justice. We should therefore compensate only for those welfare deficits which are not appropriately traceable to the individual's choices.' One reason why we should not compensate 'extravagants' for welfare deficits which are the result of their free choices, is that it encourages greed and excess, something we want to discourage in the interests of promoting social welfare. See also Baron (1993:147): 'Desires for "obscene luxuries", however strong they may be, should be discouraged because they divert resources from the satisfaction of needs that cannot be so easily controlled. The workers who cater to the wishes of the "decadent rich" could, instead, be saving the lives of the poor, or at least providing for real needs, things for which people cannot so easily reduce their desires. Of course, we can go too far in taxing the rich. Tolerance of some obscene luxuries might be a worthwhile price to pay for a system of

incentive that encourages economic production.' See also Rakowski (1997:243–4).

14   This shows, incidentally, that utilitarianism is not satisfactorily captured in the dictum 'the greatest good of the greatest number'. This contains two desiderata which may pull in opposite directions. In the present example, helping the single individual will promote the greatest good (measured on a cost-per-QALY basis), but helping the seven individuals will benefit the greatest number. Utilitarianism requires us to maximize good. Helping the greatest number is a distributional rule which will often help to achieve this end, but it is not an essential part of utilitarianism.

15   Furthermore, different people will make a whole series of trade-offs between different groups, depending on the number of people that can be saved and the length of time for which their deaths can be postponed. It is only when one side of the trade-off is held constant that it makes sense to talk about a threshold. For example, we might ask questionnaire respondents to consider one person gaining 10 years of life, and then ask them whether 10 people gaining one year of life is equivalent to this, or 20 people gaining six months, or 30 people gaining four months, and so on. This might give us a threshold, but only because one side of the equation is held constant. So there is not really just one threshold, but a whole series of them governing a series of trade-offs.

16   We will see in Chapter 5 that Harris has strong objections to utilitarianism and the QALY approach to health care allocation.

4 Quality of Life

There are two components to QALYs: the 'life year' part and the 'quality of life adjustment factor'. In the previous chapter we looked at some of the problems surrounding the life year part, and in this chapter we look at some of the problems concerning the quality of life part. Again, we will concentrate on problems about justice and fairness, for some critics have argued that prioritizing health care on the basis of QALYs discriminates unfairly not only against the aged, but also against those whose conditions are the most resistant to successful treatment. Not only does the QALY approach discriminate against those with fewer remaining life years, some critics have argued, it also discriminates against those afflicted with the most grievous illnesses and injuries, because the lower an individual's anticipated quality of life after treatment the lower their QALY score (other things being equal). Not only might the 'life year' part harbour some injustice, then, but so might the 'quality-adjusted' part.

To aid our thinking about this problem, imagine that Nora has been injured in a car accident that has left her a paraplegic. She is confined to a wheelchair and has persistent, often severe, back pain. Let us assume that two years of life in this condition is worth one year of life in good health, as determined by the 'standard gamble' or 'time trade-off'. Then Nora's quality-of-life (QoL) score is 0.5. Suppose also that her life expectancy is another 40 years, given her age and general health. Thus the number of QALYs her life would be expected to contain, if her condition remains unchanged, is 20. Suppose now that a treatment is available for Nora's back pain. Although she will still be a paraplegic (and confined to a wheelchair), and although the treatment will not change her life expectancy, the back pain will go entirely. This will raise her QoL score from 0.5 to 0.75 and the expected QALYs in her life will rise from 20 to 30.

Now compare Nora to Agnes, who was also involved in a car accident, though the injuries she sustained were less severe. If she receives no treatment, beyond the initial first aid given to her at the scene of the accident, she will be left with a limp, but will not experience any long-term pain or other disabilities as a result of her injuries. This gives her, let us suppose, a QoL score of 0.95. If her life expectancy is 40 years, like Nora's, her life would be expected to contain 38 QALYs, in the event that her condition remains unchanged. Suppose now that there is a treatment available for Agnes that will eliminate her limp completely. This would return her QoL score to 1.00 (full health) and bring her post-treatment QALY score to 40. (See Figure 4.1.)

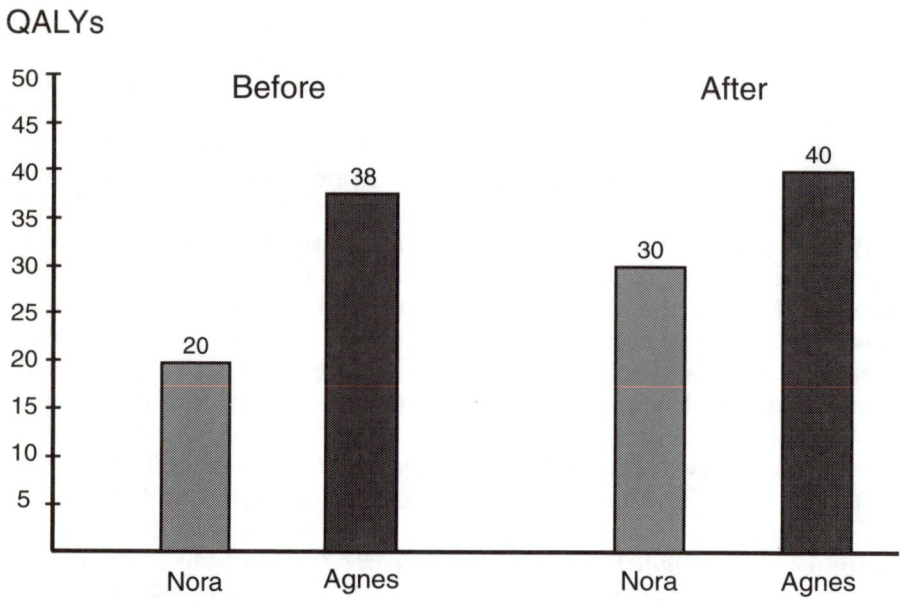

Figure 4.1   Comparative QALY gains of Nora and Agnes before and after treatment

QALY Levels and QALY Gains

Let us assume that Nora and Agnes cannot both be helped. Is it true that allocating health care resources so as to produce the largest number of QALYs (for each dollar spent) will always give Nora, the victim of the disaster that has left her permanently a paraplegic, less chance of treatment than Agnes, who has suffered a relatively minor injury? Clearly not. Although giving Agnes the treatment will leave her with a higher total number of QALYs than Nora (40 compared to 30) it would be wrong to conclude that this option is indicated by the QALY approach. If Nora receives the treatment, her post-treatment QALY score will be 30, and Agnes will stay at her pre-treatment QALY score of 38, making a total of 68 QALYs. If Agnes receives the treatment, her post-treatment QALY score will be 40, and Nora will stay at her pre-treatment QALY score of 20, making a total of 60 QALYs. Hence, although Nora, if she receives the treatment, will end up with a lower QALY score than Agnes, giving her priority is supported by QALY analysis, since it results in the largest number of QALYs overall.

The conclusion is the same if we look at the cost per QALY. For simplicity, let us suppose that Nora's and Agnes's operations cost the same, say $10 000 each. Then the $10 000 we spend on Nora brings a net gain of 10 QALYs. In other words, we have to spend $1000 for each QALY gained. By comparison, the $10 000 we spend on Agnes returns us only two QALYs, at a cost of $5000 per QALY. So if we spend our health care budget in order to maximize QALYs, we will give a higher priority to operations like those that Nora needs than to operations like those Agnes needs. Again, although Nora will end up with a lower QALY score after treatment, this is the option supported by the QALY approach.

What this shows is that, where the amelioration of a disabling or painful condition is possible, a policy of maximizing QALYs per unit cost does not systematically disadvantage the most severely injured or ill person. In the case of macro-allocation, also, if programme A will improve the health status of a group of patients X more dramatically than programme B will improve the health status of a group of patients Y (measured in terms of QALYs), for the same cost, QALY analysis indicates that programme A should have priority, regardless of whether group X can expect a poorer quality of life after treatment than group Y. In this sense, the QALY approach does not involve discrimination on the basis of quality of life.

Money for the Rich

The preceding argument only establishes that QALY maximization (per unit cost) as a decision rule does not *always* favour those who are relatively fortunate over those who are less fortunate. It remains a possibility that it *may* do so in some situations. If the preceding example involving Nora and Agnes tallies with our moral intuitions, this is no doubt in part because the option that produces the greatest number of QALYs overall is also the option of treating the least well-off party – Nora. However, this will not always be the case. Sometimes the greatest QALY gains will lie with treating those who are already better off, and this is what critics of QALY allocation are primarily objecting to when they complain that QALYs discriminate against the less fortunate.

To see this more clearly, consider another example. Imagine that Herbert needs to use a walking stick, experiences some back pain and has occasional blackouts and dizzy spells. The precise cause of these problems need not concern us. Let us suppose that his QoL score is 0.7, and that his life expectancy is 20 years, giving him a pre-treatment QALY score of 14. If he receives treatment, he will no longer have the blackouts and dizzy spells, though he will still need to use a walking stick and will experience some pain. Nevertheless, this will increase his QoL score to 0.8 and his post-treatment QALY score to 16. Waldo is in slightly better shape than Herbert. He needs to use a walking stick and experiences some back pain, but does not suffer from the blackouts and dizzy spells. This gives him a pre-treatment QoL score of 0.8. Let us assume that his life expectancy is the same as Herbert's, 20 years. This then gives him a pre-treatment QALY score of 16. However, if he receives treatment he will no longer need the walking stick or experience any pain, increasing his QoL score to 1.00, and bringing his post-treatment QALY score to 20. (See Figure 4.2.)

Imagine, further, that Herbert has had his symptoms longer than Waldo, and has therefore suffered more in the past. We might imagine that Herbert and Waldo suffer from the same condition, though Waldo has less severe symptoms, and that they both need a new treatment that has only just been developed, and can only be offered to one. Indeed, let us suppose that Herbert has had a much worse life than Waldo overall, having suffered from another painful and debilitating illness in the past that also severely affected his quality of life.

What implications does the QALY procedure have in this case? The most substantial rise in an individual QALY score will result if Waldo is given the treatment. He will go from 16 QALYs to 20 QALYs, thus gaining four QALYs. By comparison, Herbert will gain only two QALYs if he receives the treatment. Furthermore, giving the treatment to Waldo will produce the greatest number of QALYs overall. If Waldo receives the treatment, his post-treatment QALY score will be 20, and Herbert will stay at his pre-treatment QALY score of 14, making a total of 34 QALYs, whereas if Herbert receives the treatment, his post-treatment QALY score will be 16 and Waldo will stay at his pre-treatment QALY score of 16, making a total of 32 QALYs. If we are committed to allocating resources on the basis of QALYs, therefore, we will give the treatment to Waldo, since this will result in the greatest number of QALYs overall.[1]

QALYs

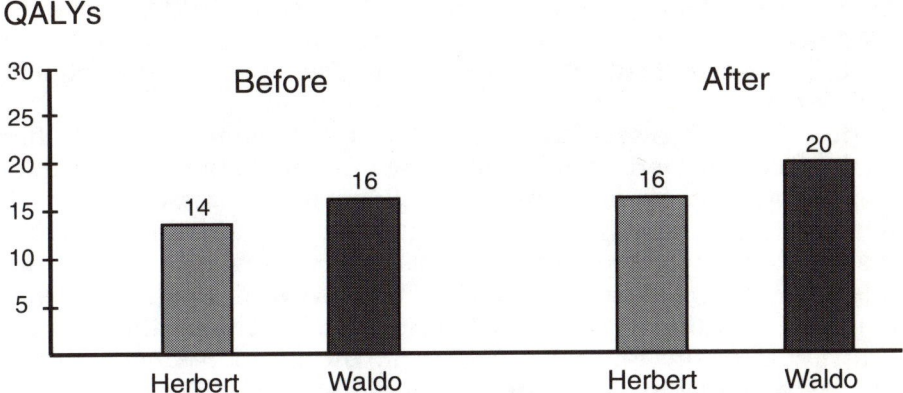

Figure 4.2   Comparative QALY gains of Herbert and Waldo before and after treatment

But it has seemed to many people that this option is not morally defensible. One reason for thinking that Herbert should really be the higher priority here lies with the fact that he is more severely affected than Waldo, not in terms of his capacity to respond to treatment but in terms of the severity of his symptoms. Not only does he need a walking stick and experience some back pain, like Waldo, but he also suffers from blackouts and dizziness. As a result, his pre-treatment QALY score is lower than Waldo's. It might therefore be thought that Herbert is more entitled to treatment on the ground that his *need* is greater: he experiences greater distress and disability.

Furthermore, if Herbert receives the treatment he will be on a par with Waldo in terms of his post-treatment QALY score. They will both have a QALY score of 16, they will both require the use of a walking stick, they will both experience some back pain, and they will both have a life expectancy of 20 years. Arguably, therefore, on grounds of equality of health outcome also, Herbert should receive the treatment. Is it not unfair to confer a substantial benefit upon Waldo, given that he is already better off, when by conferring a smaller benefit upon Herbert he can be brought to enjoy the same quality of life as Waldo, and all else is equal?

Whereas the *need objection* focuses on (comparative) pre-treatment QALY levels (Herbert should be a higher priority for treatment than Waldo because his pre-treatment QALY score is lower), the *equity objection* focuses on (comparative) post-treatment QALY levels –

Herbert should be a higher priority for treatment because this will give him the same post-treatment QALY level as Waldo. However, both objections issue in the same recommendation: contrary to the QALY approach, Herbert should be a higher priority for treatment than Waldo.

Moreover, it has seemed to some that moral significance attaches to the fact that Herbert has had his symptoms longer than Waldo, and has suffered from another major illness in the past, as a result of which he has suffered more than Waldo over his entire lifetime. From the perspective of the cost-per-QALY prioritizing rule, this is not relevant: the QALY approach is wholly forward-looking; all that matters is putting resources where they will achieve the greatest future QALY gains for each dollar spent. The idea of balancing things out, with an eye to past suffering, does not play a part. According to the *compensation objection*, however, Herbert is entitled to some special consideration because of the greater misfortune he has had to endure, through no fault of his own.

Finally, so long as the greatest QALY gain lies with treating Waldo, this will be the option indicated by the QALY procedure, regardless of the actual pre-treatment QALY scores of Waldo and Herbert. Thus someone who supports the idea that everyone should receive a decent, basic level of health care might object to the use of QALYs on the ground that Herbert would fail to receive even a decent minimum of health care if treating Waldo promised to secure more QALYs. We might call this the *'safety net'* objection.

As the first example involving Nora and Agnes makes clear, poor quality of life per se does not adversely affect the force of an individual's (or group's) claim for resources on the QALY approach. It is not really in virtue of his poor quality of life that Herbert is ruled out for treatment using QALY analysis (in comparison with Waldo). Rather, since it is overall QALY gains that are important, it is in virtue of his diminished capacity to benefit from medical intervention that he is ruled out. Nevertheless, this still means that allocation on the basis of QALYs discriminates against those whose conditions are the most resistant to successful treatment, and in consequence it may favour those who are already better off if they have conditions more amenable to successful treatment. The four objections outlined above provide plausible reasons, and for some people highly persuasive reasons, for thinking that this implication of the QALY method renders it morally unacceptable. Campbell and Gillett (1993:17) sum up this problem as it bears on the macro-allocation of health care in the following way:

> Utilitarian theories are potentially insensitive to any considerations of fairness. For instance, a Utilitarian would not necessarily see a prob-

lem in providing a health care system which took good care of middle-class urban dwellers (MUDs) but neglected other groups as long as the amount of good it did for the MUDs exceeded what would result from a more equitable provision. This obviously unfair arrangement would be justified because health care resources would have been allocated in a manner that maximised the overall benefit of society even though those who benefited within that maximisation were a restricted group.

The Compensation Objection

What can we say about the above four reasons for thinking that Herbert should be a higher priority for treatment than Waldo? Do they require that we abandon the QALY method, or that it be modified in some fundamental way? We begin with the compensation objection, which focuses on the fact that Herbert has had his symptoms longer than Waldo and has suffered from another major illness in the past. The capacity of human beings to redress an inequitable distribution of misery in the world is limited, but when the opportunity arises to equalize things to some degree – to distribute the burden more evenly – it is right to do so, according to the compensation objection. This is the quality-of-life version of the 'fair innings' argument: when it can be avoided, people should not have to endure more than their 'fair share' of human suffering.

This position is supported by Kappel and Sandøe, who distinguish between two different views concerning the span of time within which it is proper to compare the QALY gains and losses of different people (1992:313):

The life-time view sees equality as something that concerns a whole life-time. To value the lives of two persons equally we should aim at distributing resources so that each in his life viewed as a whole will have his fundamental interests fulfilled to the same degree as the other person.

The present time view sees equality as something that concerns the present moment. To value the lives of two persons equally we should at any time aim at distributing resources so that they get their actual fundamental interests fulfilled to the same degree.

Kappel and Sandøe support the lifetime view: because Herbert has suffered more than Waldo (considering their lives as wholes, including the past) he is deserving of special consideration when it comes to treatment that will improve his subsequent quality of life. To treat people equally we should distribute resources so that each person's fundamental interests are fulfilled to the same degree, including their interest in enjoying good health throughout the duration of their lives.

In support of the view that a person who has suffered more in the past should, for that reason, get special consideration when in competition for scarce resources, Kappel and Sandøe point out the appropriateness in other contexts of compensating people for ills that have befallen them. For example, we all think it fair if someone who works extra hours under sufferance, because their special skills are needed, is compensated in the form of extra payment or some extra time off, 'even if, when the time comes for him to be compensated, he is no worse off than other people who are not given extra money or extra time off' (ibid.:315).

However, appealing in this way to past suffering in prioritizing health care faces a significant problem: it seems to be an implication of the lifetime view that someone who is now suffering moderate or mild pain should be a higher priority for pain-relieving treatment than someone who is now suffering intense pain if the former has suffered more in the past (provided that their past suffering is greater than the anticipated suffering of the latter person, should they fail to receive treatment). In other words, it is an implication of the lifetime view that, under certain circumstances, someone at present suffering less should be helped in preference to someone at present suffering more, as a result of what has happened in the past. As Kappel and Sandøe acknowledge, 'this seems counterintuitive' (ibid.).

Kappel and Sandøe are not deterred by this objection to their view, however. They suggest that the intuition in favour of helping the person who is currently suffering more may reflect the fact that moderate and mild pain are comparatively tolerable without treatment, whereas intense pain must be treated unless the person is going to suffer badly. In support of this, they suggest that if the difference in degree of suffering is lessened we are more inclined to favour the person suffering least, if they have suffered more in the past: 'Imagine that both persons suffer from intense pain but the pain of the first patient is just slightly more intense than the pain of the other patient. In that case it seems more reasonable to treat the person that earlier suffered the most pain' (ibid.).

However, in giving credence to the intuition that, when the difference in degree of suffering is slight it is more reasonable to treat the person who earlier suffered the most pain, Kappel and Sandøe could be accused of begging the question. To the extent that the purpose of medical treatment is to prevent and reduce pain and suffering, and to the extent that nothing humanly possible can be done to lessen past pain and suffering, it would seem more reasonable to treat the person who is at present suffering more, since at least this person's suffering can be lessened. Nothing can be done about past suffering, whereas (often) something can be done about present and future suffering.[2] This does not mean that we should callously disregard past suffering. On the contrary, with the passage of time, present suffering becomes past suffering. Therefore the best way, indeed, the only way, to minimize (what will be) past suffering is to minimize present and future suffering. If this is correct – if our efforts should be directed at the prevention of present and (therefore) future suffering – it would seem that the compensation objection, at least as formulated by Kappel and Sandøe, does not provide a persuasive reason for abandoning the QALY approach. The compensation objection is backward looking, whereas the QALY approach is forward-looking.[3]

The Equity Objection

Consider now the equity objection. According to this objection, Herbert should receive the treatment in preference to Waldo because this will result in both him and Waldo having the same QALY score of 16, whereas giving the treatment to Waldo will merely increase the gap separating him from Herbert by another four QALYs. Giving the treatment to Waldo will thus make an unjust situation even more unjust. What we should try to do, if we are persuaded by the equity objection, is secure a more equitable distribution of benefits and harms.

Notice that this objection goes beyond the claim that, other things being equal, the more inequality there is, the worse an outcome is. This is compatible with the disvalue of the inequality being outweighed by an increase in welfare for all concerned. Rather, the equity objection holds that equality is worth pursuing even at the expense of sacrificing an increase in the overall well-being of people. Only in this form does it constitute a rival to the QALY approach. So, according to the equity objection, there is value in the relationships between people, and not just in people's lives themselves. Equality and inequality are themselves of moral significance, over and above the benefits and harms experienced by individuals (see McKerlie, 1996:275).

Economic equality can be achieved in three general ways: by raising the poor to the level of the rich, by reducing the rich to the level of the poor, or by a combination of the two so that the rich and the poor meet somewhere in the middle. But the second and third of these options are non-starters when it comes to health care allocation. No one would seriously advocate that, in the interests of achieving equality, Waldo should be given a drug that will induce occasional blackouts and dizzy spells, if this is the cheaper option, so that he will have the same QALY score as Herbert. For the same reason, improving Herbert's health and reducing Waldo's health in order to reduce the gap between them is unacceptable: it still involves harming Waldo. To be at all plausible, the equity objection must be interpreted as directing us to seek equality by raising up those who are worst off, even if this means that benefits may not be maximized.

So the idea that there is value in the relationships between lives, independently of the gains and losses individuals may undergo, must nevertheless be constrained by another principle prohibiting the achievement of equality by harming people. The equity objection, interpreted plausibly, must maintain that there are acceptable and unacceptable ways of achieving equality: an unequal outcome is *not* improved if the better-off are simply reduced to the level of the worst-off (in the case of health care, if they are directly harmed), whereas an unequal outcome *is* improved if the worst-off are raised to the level of the better-off, even when this involves sacrificing an increase in the overall well-being of people. On this view, although there is value in the relationships between lives, what happens in individual lives in the pursuit of equality – the benefits and harms people experience – is also relevant.

Furthermore, it would seem that we must allow that sometimes it is acceptable even to increase inequality. For example, if someone is beyond all help, if there is no way of improving their condition at all, it would be wrong not to help someone else who is in a position to benefit. If Herbert could not be helped at all, for instance, it would be right to help Waldo, even though the QALY gap separating them would thereby be increased.[4] So the goal of reducing inequality must be constrained not only by a principle prohibiting the achievement of this by harming those who are better off, but also by a principle allowing increases in inequality if the worst-off are not thereby disadvantaged – if they are not required to forgo a potential benefit (cf. Rawls, 1971:151). Nevertheless, this still means that there may be times when it is justifiable to pursue equality at the expense of maximizing welfare: namely, when it can be achieved by helping those who are worst off.

But as McKerlie notes (1996:288), this seems to leave equality behind as a goal in itself. The goal is not the achievement of equality as such, since inequality can justifiably be increased if the worst-off cannot be helped, and the pursuit of equality is prohibited when it can only be achieved by harming the better-off. This raises the suspicion that the real goal is not the achievement of equality as such, but helping the worst-off: 'our real objection may be to the fact that the badly off are being deprived of benefits, benefits that they would receive if the inequality was eliminated' (ibid.). Helping the worst-off will decrease inequality, but the aim is helping the worst-off, not eliminating the inequality: 'That is why we only eliminate the difference when it *does* benefit the badly off' (ibid.). The equity objection, then, if it is to have any plausibility, must be deemed to be equivalent to the need objection, which we consider in the next section.

The Need Objection

Rawles argues that, rather than allocating health care resources on the basis of QALYs, 'a more equitable system of rationing health care would be based on need' (1989:147). Similarly, Lockwood points out that 'the QALY arithmetic is inherently insensitive to differences in degree of need, except in so far as they happen to correlate with the degree of benefit per unit cost that treatment can confer' (1988:45–6). Likewise, Aday *et al.* suggest that 'the greatest "equity" of access is said to exist when need, rather than structural (for example, availability of physicians), or individual (for example, family income) factors determine who gains entry to the health care system' (Aday *et al.* 1980:26).

If we think of those in greatest need as the worst-off, we can give the need objection more substance and precision by appealing to Rawls's theory of justice, which ties the idea of justice closely to the idea of helping the worst-off members of society.[5] Rawls encapsulates his theory of justice as fairness in the following two principles (Rawls, 1971:302–3):

First Principle
Each person is to have an equal right to the most extensive total system of equal basic liberties compatible with a similar system of liberty for all.

Second Principle
Social and economic inequalities are to be arranged so that they are both:
  (a) to the greatest benefit of the least advantaged, and
  (b) attached to offices and positions open to all under conditions of fair equality of opportunity.

Rawls also provides rules according to which the first principle has priority over the second (liberty can be restricted only for the sake of liberty) and clause (b) has priority over clause (a) in the second principle. Note that the second principle does not preclude inequalities; it permits inequalities that are to the benefit of all. For example, allowing wealthier people to buy expensive surgical procedures to which others cannot gain access might allow physicians to become more experienced in the techniques required, and thus reduce the cost to an affordable level, so that everyone benefits (cf. Rawls, 1971:78; Campbell and Gillett, 1993:16; Buchanan, 1989:319).

We can now construe the clash between the QALY approach and the need objection as a clash between the utilitarianism underlying the QALY approach (we should allocate resources to those who can benefit most from them) and clause (a) of Rawls's second principle of justice, which he calls the *difference principle* (we should allocate resources to those who are worst-off, unless another distribution will benefit them even more).[6] On the face of it, these two principles are incompatible, in the sense that they may issue in diametrically opposed recommendations in some cases. If we believe that the goal of resource allocation should be to maximize QALYs, we are implicitly accepting that the value of a benefit depends on its size rather than on who receives it, whereas, according to the need objection, the value of a benefit may differ depending on who receives it – in particular, on their degree of need. 'Thinking of these differences, an egalitarian might say that the utilitarian view ignores the moral importance of the difference between lives while the egalitarian principle respects its importance' (McKerlie, 1988:207).[7]

Williams (1988:117) objects to need as a criterion of allocation on the ground that it leaves unresolved the issue of how one person's needs are to be weighed against another's. Similarly, Hope *et al.* (1993:380) ask: 'If the total resources are insufficient to meet all needs then how does one choose the needs that should take precedence?' One solution to this problem, however, is to explicate need in terms of QALY levels.[8] If Herbert has a lower pre-treatment QALY score than Waldo, he is in greater need; he is suffering more, for example, or is more severely disabled. Understood in this way, the idea of comparing the needs of different people is no more suspect than the idea of comparing the QALY levels of different people. (Rawles, for example, explicates need as 'degree of suffering' (1989:147).) Where allocation on the basis of need and allocation on the basis of QALYs differ is in their respective principles of allocation: the aim of the QALY approach is to gain the most QALYs (given economic constraints), regardless of how they are distributed; whereas, if we choose to allocate on the basis of need, the aim is to secure more QALYs for those who have fewer, even if this means that QALYs may thereby not be maximized.[9]

The Moral Arbitrariness of Ill Health

A common argument in favour of allocating resources to those in greater need focuses on the arbitrariness of good and bad health.[10]

Herbert is not responsible for the ill health from which he suffers; it is a matter of sheer bad luck, and he should not be disadvantaged because of it. Given that preventing his ill health is now no longer an option, the best way to ensure that the morally arbitrary fact of ill health does not interfere with Herbert's capacity to get the most out of his life – or interferes with it as little as possible – is to allocate resources to him preferentially. In this way the influence of totally arbitrary (and therefore morally irrelevant) factors can be minimized.

Ultimately, however, this argument begs the question, for Waldo's health is also a matter of luck. Why should he forgo an even bigger potential gain than that facing Herbert, just because he is relatively better off? Is this not a case of the morally arbitrary fact of (comparatively) *good* health interfering with Waldo's capacity to get the most out of *his* life? If there are reasons why Herbert should be a higher priority than Waldo, they will not focus on the arbitrariness of their respective health profiles, since this is common to Herbert and Waldo alike. (We leave aside self-inflicted conditions, such as lung cancer due to smoking, which are not an issue here.)

Needs, Benefits and Impartiality

In fact, on the basis of the foregoing, it might be argued that resources should be allocated to achieve the greatest surplus of benefits over harms, rather than to benefit the most needy. As individuals, we are often willing to undergo some unpleasantness in the short term for a greater gain later on. If it is acceptable to make these trade-offs between different stages of our own life, why is it not acceptable to make them between different individuals, or groups of individuals? 'If it is rational for me to choose the pain of a visit to the dentist in order to prevent the pain of toothache, why is it not rational for me to choose a pain for Jones, similar to that of my visit to the dentist, if that is the only way in which I can prevent a pain, equal to that of my toothache, for Robinson?' (Smart, in Smart and Williams 1973:37). Perhaps it is right to require a sacrifice of Herbert, even though he is in greater need (that is, require that he forgo relief from the blackouts and dizzy spells) in order that a greater benefit can accrue to Waldo (that is, that he regain full health). So long as the gain outweighs the sacrifice, individuals will make such trade-offs in their own life. So why should it be any different between individuals?

But is it true that in our own lives we would always make such trade-offs? Would it necessarily be irrational to forgo two years of intense pleasure if this could only be achieved by enduring a few months of significant suffering – say, being paralysed or in pain? Someone might prefer life on a more even keel, even if this meant that life overall would be less intensely pleasurable. But then for such a person life on a more even keel, although less intensely pleasurable overall, is preferable. For such a person, failing to endure several months of significant suffering to gain two years of intense pleasure is not irrational; this person has other goals (life on a more even keel) that he values more than the suffering and the pleasure combined. So he is not forgoing a big benefit for the sake of a smaller benefit, which would indeed display a lack of concern for his own best interests. But, again, if it is rational for people to prefer a big benefit to a small benefit in their own lives, why should not Herbert forgo a comparatively small benefit so that Waldo can benefit greatly?

Of course, some people will still object to the idea of requiring one individual or group to make a sacrifice for the benefit of another. For example, someone might object to the idea of requiring Herbert to forgo a small benefit so that Waldo can have a big benefit, *simply because* Herbert and Waldo are different people. Although it is rational for an individual to endure unpleasantness in his own life for a greater subsequent gain, it is not acceptable to require one individual to sacrifice for the sake of another, it might be argued. However, this prompts us to ask whether there really is any moral significance in the fact that Herbert and Waldo are different people. If it is rational for an individual to make a sacrifice in his own life for a greater subsequent gain, does not the ideal of *impartiality* lead us to think that such trade-offs are acceptable between different people? Whether my present sacrifice results in a later gain to me or to you would seem to be irrelevant if we adopt the view that fulfilling my preferences is as important as fulfilling yours: if we accept that benefits and harms should be distributed *impartially*.

Perhaps individual autonomy is relevant here. When a person makes a sacrifice for a later gain in his own life, it is his choice. But when Herbert sacrifices (a potential benefit) for Waldo as a result of a health care decision – because it is demanded by economic policy – he has no choice. However, this does not advance the discussion far. If resources are limited and cannot be divided, some individuals will inevitably be disadvantaged and others advantaged. Either Waldo will get the treatment and Herbert will miss out, or Herbert will get the treatment and Waldo will miss out. Realistically, therefore, it cannot be left to individuals themselves to decide who should receive the benefit. This would expose the health system to exploitation by the powerful and greedy, and more often than not would result in an impasse, with all parties wanting as much as they can get.

On the other hand, if the fact that Herbert and Waldo are different people is not of moral significance, and the only way for Waldo to gain the greater benefit is by Herbert forgoing the lesser benefit, is it not acceptable that the sacrifice be made? In support of this position, Smart claims (Smart and Williams, 1973:63):

If it were known to be true, as a question of fact, that measures which caused misery and death to tens of millions today *would* result in saving from greater misery and from death hundreds of millions in the future, and if this were the only way in which it could be done, then it *would* be right to cause these necessary atrocities. The case is surely no different in principle from that of the battalion commander who sacrifices a patrol to save a company.[11]

But the relevance of this observation to the example of Herbert and Waldo is open to dispute. Even if we concede that it would be right for Herbert to forgo a potential benefit or undergo some misery in order to prevent an even greater harm befalling Waldo, it does not follow that Herbert should forgo some benefit in order that Waldo can achieve *an even greater benefit*, given that Waldo is already better off. Giving the treatment to Waldo will not avoid a greater misfortune befalling him than will be avoided if Herbert receives the treatment, if this is understood in terms of their relative QALY levels after treatment: if Waldo does not receive the treatment, and Herbert does, they will be on a par in terms of their QALY levels; if Waldo does receive the treatment he will be substantially better off than Herbert. Under no circumstances will he be worse off than Herbert.

Sacrifices and Complaints

It may be wrong to concentrate on QALY levels here rather than overall QALY gains. Although giving the treatment to Waldo will not avoid a greater misfortune befalling him than will be avoided if Herbert receives the treatment, if this is understood in terms of their relative QALY levels after treatment, still, giving the treatment to Waldo will avoid a greater misfortune in the sense that he will be forgoing a greater potential gain if he does not receive the treatment. Waldo will forgo a potential gain of four QALYs if he does not receive treatment, whereas Herbert will only forgo a gain of two QALYs. In this sense, a greater misfortune *is* avoided by giving the treatment to Waldo.[12]

Another way of looking at this is in terms of complaints. In a situation in which some are worse off than others, who has a legitimate complaint? Temkin (1993:19–27) suggests two possible answers (among others). According to the first, only those *worse off than the average* have a complaint, because they have received less than an equal share and thus less than a fair share. Moreover, those who are better off than the average have received a fair share or more than their fair share, and therefore have nothing to complain about. According to the second answer, *all but the very best off* have a complaint. For example, if A is paid $60 for the same work for which B is paid

$100, A has a complaint. If A is paid $40 dollars for the same work for which B is paid $100, he has an even greater complaint. According to the second answer, this is so even if A is one among many who are paid $40, and is therefore receiving pay closer to the average; that is, if $40 is closer to the average than $60. So A's complaint is determined by comparing him to B, not to the average.

However, these answers focus exclusively on comparisons between individuals and make no mention of any independent measure of good. (We might say that they are concerned exclusively with equality rather than with justice more broadly construed.) Moreover, they look at individuals statically, in terms of their existing situation, rather than dynamically, in terms of what they stand to gain or lose as a result of reallocation. A third possible answer to the question of who has a legitimate complaint, then, is the following: all those who must forgo a benefit have a complaint, and the magnitude of a person's complaint is proportional to the magnitude of the benefit they must forgo. From this perspective, Waldo has a greater complaint than Herbert, for Waldo will forgo a potential gain of four QALYs if he does not receive treatment, whereas Herbert will only forgo a gain of two QALYs. So even the best-off may have a complaint if they could be even better off.

The advantages of this third answer become clearer if we imagine that there are hundreds of Waldos who are only marginally better off than Herbert, and who are themselves, let us suppose, quite badly off. Even in this case, Rawls's difference principle would require us to help Herbert, because he is worse off, and would fail to help the hundreds of Waldos who are only slightly better off than Herbert. This sort of situation leads Temkin to comment, 'while failing to benefit the worst-off person might be somewhat unjust, requiring so many who are *themselves* badly off to lose *so much* (to be sacrificed?) for another's slight benefit would be even more unjust' (Temkin, 1993:104).

Of course, someone may want to reject the whole idea that benefits and harms undergone by different people can be compared in this way. Parfit calls the view that benefits and harms in different lives cannot cancel one another out the 'objection to balancing' (Parfit, 1984:330). A harm to one individual cannot be nullified or outweighed by a benefit to another, even if the benefit is greater than the harm. This might be interpreted as the logical claim that interpersonal comparisons of harms and benefits make no sense. However, if the interpersonal comparison of harms and benefits makes no sense, then it makes no sense to say that a big QALY gain to someone who is already well off can be morally outweighed by a smaller QALY gain to someone who is worse off, and this is what the need objection maintains (see McKerlie, 1988:210). Comparisons of harms and benefits undergone by different people must make sense, or the whole enterprise of resource allocation is in jeopardy. To be at all plausible, the 'objection to balancing' principle must be interpreted as a moral claim; that is, as the claim that, even if such comparisons do make sense, losses for the worst off cannot be outweighed morally by gains for the better off, even if the gains are greater than the losses. But, of course, there is no solution here to the conflict between the rival goals of maximizing benefit and fulfilling greater need. So interpreted, the 'objection to balancing' is merely one label for the view that the latter goal should be overriding. It puts a label on the problem rather than offers a solution to it.

Reconciling Need and Efficiency

We have already observed (p. 82) that, if health care resources are distributed to those most in need (that is, those with the lowest QALY scores) without any regard to potential QALY gains, limited health care resources could be drained away to little effect. Resources able to benefit some people significantly could be siphoned off to utterly 'hopeless' cases with little or no prospects of improvement: those with incurable diseases facing imminent death, patients in a persistent vegetative state, severely multiply handicapped infants, and so on. It would seem, then, that we must abandon Rawls's difference principle as a strategy for distributing resources in the health domain, since it tells us *always* to arrange inequalities in such a way that they are to the greatest benefit of the least advantaged, rather than maximize the sum of advantages. This is an unappealing strategy for allocating health care resources because, if we have to direct resources to the worst-off cases before we can think of using them efficiently, there will be none left for those who can benefit significantly from them.[13]

However, the need objection can be interpreted as claiming, more modestly than this criticism allows, that it is *sometimes* right to direct resources to those in greater need rather than place them where they will maximize QALYs' per unit cost. It need not be interpreted as claiming that this is *always* right, even if it results in squandering resources to little or no effect. Perhaps, then, there should be a trade-off between producing the greatest QALY gains (given budget constraints) and alleviating the suffering of those most in need. This type of approach is taken by Sen:

> it is reasonable to argue that, in making ethical judgements on distributional issues (and in other types of social choices as well), one is typically concerned *both* with comparisons of levels of welfare as well as with comparisons of welfare gains and losses. It is not surprising

> that the utilitarian approach and ... [Rawls's] approach both run into some fairly straightforward difficulties since each leaves out completely one of the two parts of the total picture. (Sen, 1989:292)

However, there is an obvious problem with this view: it is quite unclear how the trade-off between these two, apparently incompatible, principles is to be effected. As Sen observes, 'a more complete theory is yet to emerge' (ibid.). In particular, if we grant that sometimes we should distribute resources efficiently (so as not to seriously squander them), but sometimes we should give resources to those who need them most (even if this is not the most efficient way to use them), this raises the problem of determining which of these imperatives is trumps on any given occasion. The 'reconciliationist' view – that we should in some circumstances allocate resources to achieve the most good, and in others to benefit the most needy, without one goal dominating to the exclusion of the other – like all ethical theories that posit a plurality of first principles, fails to give practical guidance when these principles conflict: at best, we are left to rely on 'intuition'.

By contrast, utilitarianism (and by implication the QALY method) provides one principle for all occasions: maximize utility (or QALYs). In theory, therefore, there is no uncertainty about which is the rational choice between any two actions, laws or institutions: it is that which is expected to maximize overall good:

> Therefore under all conceivable conditions, there is a uniquely rational, hence right, thing to do. Granted, it may not be knowable by us, but the idea of maximising the good provides a way to assign a truth value to any statement about what persons or groups ought to do. No other conception of rationality offers such practical completeness. (Freeman, 1994:315–16)[14]

This virtue accrues to the QALY approach also, because the QALY approach is utilitarianism applied in the health area, where the goal is to gain the maximum number of QALYs for each dollar spent, and therefore, by implication, to maximize the satisfaction of preferences (assuming that QALYs accurately reflect people's preferences). The unity and coherence of the QALY approach is threatened, however, if we concede (as the need objection requires us to concede) that on unspecified occasions (perhaps guided by 'intuition') we should abandon the goal of distributing health care resources in a way that will achieve the most good, and instead give them to those who can benefit less from them. Furthermore, refusing to allocate resources in a way that would do less good than might otherwise have been done is a bulwark against the influence of pressure groups and others who would exploit the health care system for their own benefit. The QALY approach is often criticized for being inegalitarian, but, as we have noted, allocating resources in a way that maximizes human well-being, giving equal weight to each person's interests in the process, is an expression of our refusal to allocate resources in a biased way, and reflects our commitment to impartiality.[15]

The 'Safety Net' Objection

The 'safety net' objection to QALY-based allocation focuses on the fact that, so long as the greatest QALY gains lie with treating Waldo, he will be a higher priority for treatment than Herbert regardless of their actual pre-treatment QALY scores. Potentially, therefore, the cost-per-QALY prioritizing rule conflicts with the idea that everyone should receive a decent, basic level of health care. On the QALY approach, Herbert might fail to receive even a minimum of help.

Support for the idea of a safety net to protect individuals from significant, unexpected misfortune would appear to be common and widespread. For example, Frohlich and Oppenheimer conducted empirical research, in several different cultural settings, on what people think is a just distribution of income (Frohlich and Oppenheimer, 1992). They found that subjects wanted to maximize the average income only after a certain specified minimum income is guaranteed to everyone:

> Groups generally chose a floor constraint. The groups wanted an income floor to be guaranteed to the worst-off individual. This floor was to act as a safety net for all individuals. But after this constraint was set, they wished to preserve incentives so as to maximise production and hence average income. (Frohlich and Oppenheimer, 1992:59)

Beauchamp and Childress also outline arguments in favour of the idea of a health care safety net. Firstly, they note that good governments assume responsibility for protecting their citizens from threats presented by crime, fire, pollution, and so on. Why should this not be extended to collective social protection from threats to health? Protection from threats to health from illness and injury would seem to be at least as essential as protection from environmental and criminal threats: 'Consistency suggests that essential health care assistance in response to threats to health should like-wise be a collective responsibility' (Beauchamp and Childress, 1994:351–5). Secondly, according to Beauchamp and Childress, justice requires that health care resources be used to counteract the disadvantaging effects of illness, injury and disease. But protection from catastrophic and chronic illness, injury and disease cannot be left to private funding; it is too expensive. Thus the government has an obligation to provide a decent minimum of health care: health care 'at the level needed for persons to receive as fair a chance in life as possible' (ibid.:352). (Cf. also Fried, 1976; Brandt, 1959:424–7.)

The QALY approach would face a serious problem if it was in principle incompatible with protection from serious threats to health: if it was incompatible with the very idea of a health care safety net. But it is not. To see this it is helpful to consider a distinction Hare makes between Rawls's strategy of maximizing the welfare of the worst-off, on the one hand, and insuring against utter calamity, on the other. Hare notes that 'we insure our houses against fire because we think that a certain outcome, namely having one's house burnt down and having no money to buy another, is so calamitous that we should rule it out' (Hare, 1975:104–5). What lesson can we derive from this about the allocation of health resources in a competitive environment? At best it supports the idea that, *below a certain level*, the interests of the more advantaged can be sacrificed to those of the less advantaged. It does not support such sacrifice in general. As Hare notes, Rawls's strategy yields principles of justice,

> according to which it would always be just to impose any loss, however great, upon a better-off group in order to bring a gain, however small, to the least advantaged group, however affluent the latter's starting point. If intuitions are to be used, this is surely counterintuitive; at least, not many of us are as egalitarian as that. (Ibid.:107)

So the strategy of insuring against utter calamity, for which Hare has some sympathy (ibid.:105),[16] should not be identified with the strategy of seeking the best worst outcome in general, as Rawls advocates. The former is possible without the latter: at a minimum, then, we are not endorsing Rawls's difference principle if we accept the idea of a health care safety net.

However, this will give little comfort to a supporter of QALYs, for prima facie it is incompatible with the QALY approach to claim that it is *ever* right to direct resources away from those who can benefit most from them, even if those resources are thereby channelled to another group who fall below a minimum standard. So there appears to remain an incompatibility between QALY-based allocation and the idea of a health care safety net. But two things can be said here in support of the QALY approach. First, in the real world, the QALYs sacrificed by those who are already relatively healthy, by forgoing resources, would tend to be less than the QALYs gained by those who would benefit from the existence of a health care safety net. Notice that this is a utilitarian justification for helping the worse-off – a justification based on maximizing health gains – rather than a reason for invariably helping the most needy. Second, even if this were not so (even if the QALYs forgone by the more healthy group outnumbered the QALYs gained by those protected by the safety net) it might be possible to justify the existence of a decent minimum of health care by appealing to its potential for increasing social welfare more generally. Arguably, a world in which the unfortunate are looked after is better overall than a world in which they are not, other things being equal. Without the safety net a whole section of the community may feel they are being unfairly treated because of circumstances beyond their control: because they lost out in the 'natural lottery' that determines health. If they become sufficiently disgruntled, community support for the health care system may erode, and a general decrease in social welfare might result. There might be widespread feelings of resentment and envy in the community, whereas a safety net might reasonably be expected to reinforce feelings of security and trust, as a result of the belief that social arrangements are fair.

This justification of a decent minimum of health care should not be construed as an attempt to reconcile utilitarianism with the difference principle. It should not be confused with the aim of helping those most in need because they are most in need. Rather, it is a recognition that helping those most in need might be the best way of maximizing social welfare. According to Sen, 'The utilitarian procedure is based on comparing *gains and losses* to different persons (e.g. "person 1 gains more from this change than person 2 loses"), and is completely insensitive to comparisons of *levels* of welfare (e.g. "person 1 is better off than person 2")' (Sen, 1989:284). But this is not so: utilitarianism is sensitive to comparisons of levels of welfare to the extent that they have consequences for the gains and losses people undergo. So in order to justify a decent minimum of health care it is not necessary to posit two first principles (utilitarianism and the difference principle) between which we must somehow effect a choice on different occasions (perhaps with the guidance of 'intuition'); rather, the goal of maximizing social welfare can be seen as paramount, and as justifying the goal of helping those in greater need.[17]

The safety net objection is really a specific form of the need objection: those who 'need' resources are those who would suffer were the safety net not in place. And the same problem of potential wastage that faced the need objection also faces the safety net objection: if everyone is entitled to a decent minimum of health care, regardless of their prospects for improvement, this must include the most 'hopeless' cases also. But few people would deny that it is wrong to waste limited resources on utterly futile treatments, if patients who can benefit significantly from those resources will miss out. We must be mindful then that, just as the goal of maximizing the well-being of the community can justify the existence of a decent minimum of health care in the appropriate circumstances, so it can justify withholding resources from those whose prospects for improvement are so bad that resources would be wasted.

Finally, if we accept the need for a health care safety net, the obvious problem arises of where we should place it. What exactly constitutes a decent minimum of health care? Depending on how this 'should' is understood, this might be interpreted as a moral or a practical problem. A defender of the QALY method who sees it as an expression of utilitarianism in the health domain, as an attempt to satisfy people's preferences for health, has a ready answer to the moral question: the exact placement of the safety net is determined by the principle of utility maximization. The aim of maximizing social welfare should tell us whether a safety net is warranted at all, and if so where it should be placed. This leads, of course, to the practical problem of determining what policies will in fact increase social welfare. Although this is a difficult problem, it does not call into question the QALY approach. Most critics of the QALY approach will agree that at some point we must take into account the efficient use of our resources: we must attempt to determine whether a particular allocation decision increases or decreases welfare, if only as a part of what we must do. It would seem, then, that the problem of determining what policies will in fact increase social welfare is a problem that confronts any reasonable theory of resource allocation, and not just the QALY approach. Knowing where to place a health care safety net depends upon knowing how different allocation decisions will affect social welfare, and this is a general problem extending beyond the QALY method per se.

Notes

1   We are dealing with single individuals in these examples, for ease of exposition, but the same point holds generally: a group which is already better off may be given priority over a group which is worse off, if this will maximize QALYs per unit cost.

2   Of course, it is possible that the experience of past pain can influence the experience of present pain. A long period of unremitting pain can lead to exhaustion and therefore reduce our capacity to cope with present pain. But giving such a patient priority can be justified on the ground that their *present* pain is more distressing, rather than on the ground that they have experienced more pain in the past.

3   Kappel and Sandøe's example of compensating someone in the form of extra payment or time off for extra hours worked is also amenable to a forward-looking interpretation. We reward someone who works extra hours under sufferance in the hope that this will encourage similar behaviour in the future, either from the individual concerned or from others.

4 The only other alternative is levelling down: if the condition of the worst-off cannot be improved at all, and we are committed to equality, we would have to reduce the best-off to the level of the worst-off. See Pojman and Westmoreland (1997:5). 'No doubt egalitarians would like to raise everyone up to the highest level, but with regard to many qualities this seems impossible. Given the present technology there is no way we can raise imbeciles to the level of Einsteins or valetudinarians to the level of optimal health or the blind to the ability level of the sighted, so that the "thoroughgoing egalitarian", if equality is a transcendent value, as Jencks would have it, would have to dumb down the brilliant, infuse the healthy with disease, and blind the sighted.'

5 In fact, this involves a significant extrapolation of Rawls's views. Rawls has been criticized precisely for not allowing natural (as opposed to social) inequalities, such as those arising from health status, to be a factor in determining who is worse off and therefore more deserving of compensation. Note Kymlicka: 'According to Rawls, people born into a disadvantaged class or race not only should not be denied social benefits, but also have a claim to compensation because of that disadvantage. Why treat people born with natural handicaps any differently? Why should they not also have a claim to compensation for their disadvantage (e.g. subsidized medicine, transportation, job training, etc.), in addition to their claim to non-discrimination?' (Kymlicka, 1990:72–3). However, Martin (1985:180) and Pogge (1989:189) suggest that this criticism is misguided, since Rawls's theory of justice is about 'fundamental justice', whereas compensation for natural disadvantages is about 'the overall fairness of the universe'. But as Kymlicka points out, 'neither author explains this contrast, nor how it is consistent with Rawls's emphasis on "mitigating the effects of natural accident and social fortune"' (1990:92, n 5).

6 As Elster points out (1991:117), this clash is not uncommon: 'Should schools, for instance, allocate extra resources – smaller classes or additional equipment – to the least gifted or to the most gifted children? Should agencies for the mentally retarded give priority to those who are so severely retarded that they are unlikely to enjoy life much under any circumstances, or to those who can benefit substantially from supportive measures? Should agencies for rehabilitation of prisoners give priority to recalcitrant high-risk or to more promising low-risk cases?'

7 Rawls also raises this criticism: 'The most natural way, then, of arriving at utilitarianism (although not, of course, the only way of doing so) is to adopt for society as a whole the principle of rational choice for one man ... . It is this spectator who is conceived as carrying out the required organization of the desires of all persons into one coherent system of desire; it is by this construction [of the impartial spectator] that many persons are fused into one.... Utilitarianism does not take seriously the distinction between persons' (1971:26–7).

8 Another possibility is to follow Daniels and explicate need in terms of 'normal species functioning', but we have already seen (pp. 55–9) that this notion is too vague to be helpful.

9 A qualification is needed to the claim that the worst-off should be given priority over the better-off, on the need approach. A person in greater need should not be a higher priority for treatment over someone in lesser need if a greater inequity will thereby result. Herbert should receive the treatment only if the post-treatment QALY gap separating him from Waldo will not be made *greater* than the previous QALY gap separating them in favour of Waldo. (See Harris, 1994:77.)

10 This is an extension of Rawls's idea that distributive shares should not be influenced by factors like the distribution of natural talents and social contingencies. See Rawls (1971:72–5).

11   Smart is not eager to recommend such measures, however. He rightly points out how uncertain the remote effects of our actions are: 'One thing we should now know about the future is that large-scale predictions are impossible' (Smart and Williams, 1973:64).

12   Utilitarianism is often criticized on the ground that, in the pursuit of maximizing good, it may require sacrifices of one group 'for the sake of another'. This is often contrasted with Rawls's difference principle, which only allows social and economic inequalities which are to the benefit of the least advantaged: 'Each person possesses an inviolability founded on justice that even the welfare of society as a whole cannot override ... . It does not allow that the sacrifices imposed on a few are outweighed by the larger sum of advantages enjoyed by many' (Rawls, 1971:3–4). But as Nagel (1975:12–14) and Scanlon (1975:198–9) point out, Rawls's difference principle requires sacrifices no less than utilitarianism. In a society governed by the difference principle, those who are *better off* will be asked to accept less than they might otherwise have had 'for the sake of others'. Rawls is aware of this, but defends the difference principle on the ground that it expresses 'an undertaking to regard the distribution of natural abilities as a collective asset so that the more fortunate are to benefit only in ways that help those who have lost out' (Rawls, 1971:179). However, as Scanlon points out (1975:201), this begs the question against the utilitarian alternative, which holds: 'Any asset one may have control over, whether a personal talent or a transferable good, one is bound to disburse in such a way as to make the greatest contribution to human well-being.' If Rawls's difference principle is preferable to the utilitarian principle, it cannot be because the latter requires sacrifices whereas the former does not. Indeed, not only does Rawls's principle require sacrifices, it requires sacrifices of those who stand to gain most; in this sense it requires the biggest sacrifices.

13   Rawls claims in support of his account of justice as fairness that his two principles, unlike the utilitarian principle of maximizing welfare, could reasonably be expected to elicit general community support. This is so because the two principles protect the worst-off, and avoid requiring one group to make sacrifices for the benefit of another (Rawls, 1971:175–8). But it is doubtful that the two principles would command assent as readily as Rawls supposes. Human nature being what it is, few people would be happy to see resources, from which they or others could benefit greatly, diverted to individuals who are able to benefit from them only very little. Is there not a corresponding moral repugnance attached to the idea of doing less good – possibly significantly less good – than we might otherwise do? Rawls claims of the utilitarian system, which may demand that some should forgo advantages for the sake of the greater good of the whole, 'Thus the scheme will not be stable unless those who must make sacrifices strongly identify with interests broader than their own' (ibid.:177–8). But it is equally true that those who must forgo gains for the benefit of the worse off, as Rawls's two principles require, must 'strongly identify with interests broader than their own'.

14   See also Mill: 'whether happiness be or not be the end to which morality should be referred – that it be referred to an end of some sort and not left in the domain of vague feeling or inexplicable internal conviction, that it be made a matter of reason and calculation, and not merely of sentiment, is essential to the very idea of moral philosophy; is, in fact, what renders argument or discussion on moral questions possible' (Mill, 1962:114–15).

15   Cf. Kymlicka (who is in fact a critic of utilitarianism): 'Finding the morally right answer becomes a matter of measuring changes in human welfare, not of consulting spiritual leaders, or relying on obscure traditions ... . At its best, utilitarianism is a strong weapon against prejudice and superstition, providing

a standard and a procedure that challenge those who claim authority over us in the name of morality' (Kymlicka, 1990:11).

16 'I have no inclination to maximin [maximize the minimum level of welfare], once the acceptable minimum is assured; after that point I feel inclined to take chances in the hope of maximising my expectation of welfare, as I do in actual life (for example, I do not entirely refrain from investing my own cash because I might lose it)' (Hare, 1975:106).

17 Rescher suggests that, in order to prevent 'individual interests' being sacrificed for 'the general benefit', we need to add to the principle of utility 'another qualifying clause, a "principle of catastrophe-prevention" stipulating a minimal *utility* floor for all individuals below which no one should be pressed' (Rescher, 1966:29). Rescher conceives of this as a qualification of the utilitarian principle itself. But this raises the questions, what justifies imposing such a utility floor; and where should it be placed? Rescher cannot appeal to the utilitarian principle itself for an answer to these questions, since this would be circular: he would be appealing to the idea of a utility floor (that is, the utilitarian principle itself, which must include mention of a utility floor on Rescher's account) to justify the existence and placement of a utility floor. Less problematically, it is better to view the existence of a utility floor or safety net not as something which must be appended to the principle of utility itself – not as something which must be mentioned in the very specification of the principle – but as something that may be *justified* on utilitarian grounds.

5   Double Jeopardy

In the previous chapter we looked at cases where different individuals have different prospects for improvement in their quality of life as a result of treatment, and we asked what implications these differences have for the QALY approach. The situation is rather different when some people will experience a poorer quality of life after treatment no matter how successful the treatment is, for reasons which are unrelated to their current health problems. Imagine that Arne and Zach have been involved in car accidents and suffered injuries identical to those suffered by Nora and Agnes, respectively, with one important difference: there is no treatment that can help either Arne or Zach. For the rest of his life, Arne must expect to be confined to a wheelchair with persistent and often severe back pain; and Zach will walk with a limp for as long as he lives. If these were the only medical problems afflicting Arne and Zach, they would both have a life expectancy of 40 years. Unfortunately, however, both suffer serious heart conditions which, without treatment, will rapidly prove fatal. A heart transplant offers the only hope, at a cost of $100 000. What are the QALY implications of providing heart transplants for Arne and Zach?

For simplicity, let us assume that without the transplant each will die immediately, while with the transplant each will live for 40 years. Remember, however, that being wheelchair-bound and subject to back pain reduces Arne's quality of life score to 0.5, whereas Zach's is 0.95 since he only has a limp. So with the transplant Arne will have 20 QALYs and Zach 38. If the operation is given to Arne, each QALY gained will have cost $5000, whereas if it is given to Zach the cost per QALY gained will be only $2632. So if heart transplants are rationed on the basis of QALYs, it would appear, Zach will be a higher priority than Arne. But Harris argues that this involves a form of 'double jeopardy':

> QALYs dictate that because an individual is unfortunate, because she has once become a victim of disaster, we are required to visit upon her a second and perhaps graver misfortune. The first disaster leaves her

with a poor quality of life and QALYs then require that in virtue of this she be ruled out as a candidate for life saving treatment, or at best, that she be given little or no chance of benefiting from what little amelioration her condition admits of. (Harris, 1987:120)

The QALY approach seems to discriminate unfairly against those who, when faced with a life-threatening illness, are unfortunate enough to already have a permanent disability, because the lower an individual's anticipated quality of life after treatment the lower their QALY score (other things being equal). In this sense the permanently disabled suffer a 'double jeopardy' under the QALY approach: not only are they disabled, which is bad enough, but as a result they are disadvantaged in the competition for limited resources which may save their life if they are struck by a second illness or injury.[1]

Of course, this only forces us to ask: if our resources are limited and we cannot save every life that could be saved by some form of health care, is it really unfair to give a lower priority to saving the lives of those with incurable conditions that significantly reduce their quality of life? In answering this question, it is worth reflecting on what we would say about a patient who faced a reduced life expectancy after treatment rather than reduced quality of life. Imagine that Arne and Zach had not been involved in any accidents, but that they both still required life-saving heart transplants. Imagine further that, although he has not been involved in an accident, Arne has an entirely separate incurable medical condition which, although it causes him no problems now, will suddenly flare up and end-his life. Because of this, his life expectancy is only 20 years, whereas Zach's is almost twice this, at 38 years. Is there any relevant difference between giving a lower priority to Arne because he faces a reduced quality of life and giving him a lower priority because he faces a shorter life expectancy?

From the QALY perspective, the case where Arne faces a lower expected quality of life after treatment, and the case where he faces a shorter life expectancy, are identical. If heart transplants are being rationed on the basis of QALYs, Zach will be a higher priority in each case, because treating him is where the greatest QALY gains lie. Of course, in one case Arne loses out because he has a lower expected quality of life, whereas in the other he has a shorter expected lifespan. But, if we are merely concerned with gaining the most QALYs for our health dollar, this does not matter.

Someone may be inclined to accept QALY verdicts when a difference in life expectancy is responsible for a difference in QALY outcomes but not when the outcome is determined by differences in the quality of life, because they are more confident that a difference in life expectancy is an objective measure of something, whereas they are suspicious of attempts to put cardinal values on people's quality of life. In other words, we know that two years are twice as long as one year, but we lack conviction that a year of life in normal health is really as good as two years of life scored as 0.5. This worry is understandable. However, we all make judgments about whether the quality of our own lives has improved or worsened, about whether the quality of our children's lives would be improved by enrolling them in a different school, about whether the quality of life in developed countries is better than that in third world countries, and so on. Such judgments are sometimes difficult and complex but we cannot fail to make them in practice, and the QALY approach is currently the best theory we have that does incorporate quality of life as a factor in health care decision making. Being suspicious about attempts to measure quality of life, then, would appear not to be a sufficient reason for rejecting QALY recommendations based on differences in expected quality of life, at least until a theory comes along that is better than the QALY method at incorporating these necessary judgments into our allocation decisions.[2]

Random Allocation

On the other hand, someone may agree that the case where Arne faces a lower expected quality of life after treatment than Zach, and the case where he faces a shorter life expectancy, are essentially the same, but want to argue that in *neither* case should preference be given to one of them over the other. This is the approach taken by Harris, who argues that we should focus on the patients' desire to go on living, or desire for a better quality of life, rather than on the number of QALYs to be gained. He holds that 'the value of life can only sensibly be taken to be that value that those alive place on their lives' (Harris, 1988:93). Indeed, according to Harris, if the only difference between two patients is their quality of life or life expectancy, and both want to live, then the only way to allocate resources between them is *randomly* (if the resources cannot be divided and there is only enough for one) (see Harris, 1995:152-53). If we were to take this line consistently, we would also have to object to giving the treatment to Zach rather than Arne if they both wanted very much to live, even if the heart transplant could offer Arne only a year or two, while it still offered Zach 38 years. And, of course, the further we push this example, the more implausible it becomes. For example, it is not clear what basis Harris would have for giving the treatment to Zach rather than Arne, even if the latter would have only a month or a week to live.

Harris is aware of this problem, but he is not prepared to abandon his view, for he sees the supporter of QALY-based allocation as being vulnerable to a similar problem. Supporters of the QALY approach 'are committed to valuing lives more, the more un-elapsed lifetime they contain. This they would (or should) maintain however small this temporal advantage is, so long as it is sufficient for the particular individual to derive some benefit from it, so long as it gives him or her *some* interest in continued life derived from that temporal advantage. Likewise for small advantages in quality of life' (ibid.:155). According to Harris, 'both [sides] seem vulnerable when small differences are highlighted' (ibid.:156).

However, these situations seem to be relevantly different. It is true that someone with a slight QALY advantage, someone who faces the prospect of a slightly better quality of life or life expectancy after treatment, will be a higher priority for treatment if we allocate on a cost-per-QALY basis (if all else is equal). But it can be argued that this is appropriate: it is a sign of the sensitivity of the QALY approach, its capacity to take into account even small benefits, if they are genuine, and there are no other differences between claimants on which to base a decision; that is, all else is equal. By contrast, the 'small differences' problem confronting Harris's position is not really a 'small differences' problem at all: it is a 'big differences' problem. For example, even if the difference between what Arne will gain and what Zach will gain is huge, say 30 years of good-quality life, Harris's position, according to which we should allocate resources randomly, still cannot take account of it. The 'problem' confronting the QALY approach is one of sensitivity (that is, it can be seen as a virtue), whereas the problem confronting Harris's view is one of insensitivity: it (sometimes) cannot take account of big differences in quality of life gains and quantity of life gains. Potentially, it violates, not just in a minor way, but in a big way, the principle that we should allocate resources to achieve the most good.

Moreover, on Harris's account, we need to know whether an individual 'would like her own life to stand in equal competition with all other lives' (ibid.:152). Presumably, if a person does not have this desire, there is no obligation to count her life equally with all others. But if we had to choose between funding one of two large-scale health programmes it would be impractical to survey all of the potential beneficiaries to see whether, how and to what extent they value their lives. (It goes without saying that this would be impossible for future generations.) Presumably, on Harris's account, we would just have to assume that *everyone* 'would like their own life to stand in equal competition with all other lives'. But this jeopardizes the practicality of Harris's account. In effect, it requires us either to fund everything, which is impossible, or, again, to fund health care programmes at random. If we adopt Harris's approach we must assume that everyone is equally deserving of resources that will save their life, because in the macro-allocation context there is no way of knowing who 'would like their own life to stand in equal competition with all other lives'. This appears to involve a refusal to take even the most cursory account of efficiency in allocating resources.

The Equal Value of Lives

Harris's real objection to the QALY approach is that it entails that 'all individuals would have lives of different value' (Harris, 1995:152). There is a sense in which this is true. When we must make hard choices about who will and who will not receive health care, owing to limited resources, some people will receive those resources and some will not, or will not receive as large a share. In this sense, different lives will have different value. But the QALY approach is not unique in this respect: it is an unavoidable feature of any decision procedure for allocating resources that is not purely random, and even random allocation procedures will have the unwelcome consequence that some people will not receive care. The idea that different lives have different value, in the sense that some people will be a higher priority for health care than others, is a feature of cost–benefit analysis and cost–effectiveness analysis also – and of any theory that assumes we have responsibility for ranking the uses of our health care resources.

On the other hand, there is a sense in which the claim that 'all individuals would have lives of different value' if we use QALY maximization as the basis of allocation is not true. As we have seen, the QALY approach is egalitarian in the sense that equal weight is given to the QALYs of all those potentially affected by an allocation decision, regardless of wealth, race, social standing, gender, and so on; unless there are overriding moral reasons for attaching differential weights to some QALYs, no one's QALYs count for more than anyone else's. In this sense, all lives are of equal worth. A supporter of the QALY approach can consistently maintain that all individuals have lives of equal value in the latter sense, while at the same time holding that all individuals have lives of different value in the former sense – that some individuals should be accorded higher priority in the allocation of resources than others, in the context of resource shortages, depending on their capacity to benefit from them.

Harris also suggests that, if we use QALYs to allocate resources, there will always be a discrepancy between the estimated value of a person's life and its actual value, which in the case of life and death decisions would always be concealed: 'If Singer's life were to be saved rather than Harris's because his quality of life and life expectancy were allegedly greater, no one would ever know whether or not my life was *in "fact"* the more valuable, because I did in the event (and *per imposibile*) live longer with a bigger smile on my face' (ibid.). However, this merely reveals that human beings are not omniscient. We have to make decisions – even life and death decisions – on the basis of the best information we have available, which is often limited. From the QALY perspective, if we *must* choose between saving Singer's life and saving Harris's life, we should save the one who we *expect* will benefit most from having his life saved. The fact that we might make the wrong choice, and will never know, merely reflects our human limitations. But facing the prospect of being wrong should not deter us from making hard decisions as best we can; it should not force us into making random choices.

Harris also argues that, from the QALY perspective, the value of life would vary with the quality of an individual's life, 'so that those with greater quality would have greater value and the wrong done by murder, for example, would vary with the quality of the victim's life, the greater the quality the greater the wrong done in ending it' (ibid.). In a sense this is true. If Arne is murdered with only two days to live, the loss is less, from the QALY point of view, than if Zach is murdered with 30 years left to live, if all else is equal. And this has some plausibility. If we were faced with the prospect of having to forfeit either two days or 30 years of our own life, and we wanted to live as long as possible, we would, if rational, choose to forfeit two days. But we must be cautious about what implications we draw from this. It does not follow that the law should punish Arne's murderer less severely than Zach's murderer. If we want the law to deter murder and other forms of violent assault, if we want to engender respect for life in the community, and so on, it may be best for the law to treat the murderer of Arne no more leniently than the murderer of Zach. Of course, motives must be taken into account also. If Arne's murderer sincerely believes he is acting in Arne's best interests by sparing him from two days of suffering, then it may be entirely appropriate for the law to treat him more leniently for this reason. On the other hand, if Arne's murderer was merely taking advantage of his helplessness, the law may treat this as a particularly heinous crime. In brief, we should not draw conclusions about the justifiability of punishment merely on the basis of the victim's quality of life or life expectancy.

The Veil of Ignorance

Another way of testing the acceptability of giving lower priority to those with a poorer expected quality of life or life expectancy is to examine what our own preferences would be if we judged rationally and impartially. As we have seen (p. 13), Rawls has suggested that we can decide whether social arrangements are just by asking whether they would be agreed to by rational egoists choosing from behind a veil of ignorance (Rawls, 1971: ch. 1). The point of the veil of ignorance is that it forces an impartial choice by preventing people knowing whether they will be advantaged or disadvantaged by a proposed arrangement. So, applying Rawls's idea to health care, we imagine people choosing a basis for allocating health care without knowing whether, at some point in their lives, they will be in need of life-saving treatment; and they also do not know whether, if this happens, they will be among those whose interest in continuing to live is low, or among those whose interest is high.

How would two rational egoists choose if they were faced with a situation in which they each need life-saving treatment, and each has an interest in continued life, but there is enough life-saving treatment for only one? Obviously, being egoists, each would choose the treatment for himself or herself, if this was a possibility. But suppose that they had to make the choice behind a veil of ignorance, in which situation they knew the details of the two patients' conditions, but did not know which patient they were. What would they choose then? They would certainly not choose the option of giving the treatment to neither person, for this would mean that they would certainly die. In comparison with that prospect, tossing a coin would at least give them a 50 per cent chance of survival, and so would be preferable. But a random method would in turn seem less attractive than a method of selection that gives preference to the person with a stronger interest in continuing to live, since, if there is a 50 per cent chance of ending up dead on both the random method and the QALY method, the rational egoist will ask which method offers the greater potential gain if he or she does *not* end up dead. To maximize the satisfaction of their own interests, it would seem, rational egoists would choose a system that gives preference to saving life when it is most in the interests of the person whose life is saved. This means that if QALYs are an accurate way of measuring when life is most in one's interests – that is, if they accurately reflect people's preferences regarding health – rational egoists would choose to allocate in accordance with QALYs. If this is so, then at least by one widely accepted, and undoubtedly impartial, way of deciding on the principles of distribution, double jeopardy is not a sign of unfairness.

The Purpose of the Veil

This argument from the hypothetical consent of rational egoists undermines the suggestion that QALYs are unfair or unjust because they lead to double jeopardy. The argument is not new, however, and

Harris has raised several objections to it. The first, citing Ronald Dworkin, is that hypothetical agreement does not provide an independent argument for the fairness of the arrangement that would be agreed to (Harris, 1988:88–9). It is little more than a colourful way of presenting an argument: 'you use the device of a hypothetical agreement to make a point that might have been made without that device, which is that the solution is so obviously fair and sensible that only someone with an immediate contrary interest could disagree' (Dworkin, 1977:151). This is true, by and large, although it would be appropriate to add following the last clause, 'or someone who has fixed ideas about what constitutes "unjust discrimination" and has not reflected adequately on the implications of these ideas'. For while the device of hypothetical agreement is certainly just an expository device, it can reveal aspects of a situation that were not well understood beforehand. Such a device can bring hidden assumptions into focus and allow us to see the implications of those assumptions more clearly (cf. Kymlicka, 1990:68).

Slavery as a Counter-example

Harris further argues that, if arrangements are chosen behind a veil of ignorance, that does not ensure that they are just or impartial. He offers the example of people choosing a slave-owning society, gambling on being a member of the large number of slave-owners who enjoy living luxurious lives, rather than one of the small number of wretched slaves (Harris, 1988:89). However, it is not clear whether Harris is here talking about a world rather like our own, or one in which human nature, and other conditions, are quite different from what they are now. For example, since the difference between being a citizen in a non-slave-owning society and being a slave-owner in a slave-owning society is not so great as the difference between being a slave in a slave-owning society and being a citizen in a non-slave-owning society, at least if these two societies are otherwise much like ours, it would not be worth taking a chance of ending up as a slave. At least, it would not be rational unless our chances of ending up a slave were very small indeed. But this would not be the case. In the real world, a ratio of one slave to every 10 free people would certainly not be enough to make the lives of the slave-owners wonderfully luxurious. But again, the more slaves there are the less rational it would be to take the risk of ending up a slave. It would seem then that, if human nature, and other social conditions, are assumed to be roughly the same as they are now, rational egoists behind a veil of ignorance would not choose to allow slavery.

Harris rejects this argument, and cites the example of Aristotle against it:

Aristotle is notorious for having supported slavery, and in particular for having defended the right of the victors in battle to enslave the defeated, although he could not for sure and certain have known that he, or the Greeks, would never be defeated in battle by non-Greeks, indeed he knew that the contrary was the case … . Greek rational egoists with human nature not a million miles from our own, might well have supported slavery from behind a veil of ignorance, believing in the superiority of their own nature, or believing that those whose nature was not superior would deserve to be slaves. (Harris, 1995:154).

But there are two points that undermine this argument. Firstly, if Aristotle endorsed slavery in the knowledge that he was making his own situation worse, he was not choosing as a rational egoist. As we have noted, the more the slave-owning society is otherwise like our own, the more slaves there must be to ensure a luxurious life for the slave-owners and the more wretched the lives of the slaves must seem when compared to our own, and thus the more irrational it would be to choose slavery. In the real world, rational egoists would only support slavery if they knew for certain that they would be among the masters and not the slaves. Aristotle would really have to 'believe in the superiority of his own nature' (and believe that this would protect him from ending up a slave), which from behind a veil of ignorance he is not entitled to do. Secondly, as this last point suggests, Aristotle appears to have supported the enslavement of captives in war only in the case of inferior peoples: 'it is part of nature's plan that the art of war, of which hunting is a part, should be a way of acquiring property; and that it must be used both against wild beasts and against such men as are by nature intended to be ruled over but refuse; for that is the kind of warfare which is by nature right' (Aristotle, 1962: bk I). It is unlikely that Aristotle considered himself 'by nature intended to be ruled over', as with, for example, someone who 'participates in the reasoning faculty so far as to understand but not so as to possess it' (ibid.). Like most advocates of slavery, it seems that Aristotle supported the practice only for a group of which he did not believe himself to be a member. But again, this is a belief we cannot suppose him to have, when we imagine him behind a veil of ignorance.

Rawls's Derivation of the Difference Principle

Harris also appeals to Rawls's own attitude toward the veil of ignorance in rejecting the idea that the test supports the fairness of the QALY approach. He points out that Rawls himself holds that rational egoists behind a veil of ignorance would choose two specific principles of justice (see p. 83, above), the second of which includes the difference principle: inequalities in wealth and resources are justifiable only in so far as they operate to the advantage of the worst-off members of society. The difference principle, we have already seen, is incompatible with the idea of distributing resources in a way that maximizes QALYs per unit cost. Harris therefore argues that, if it could be shown that the device of choice behind a veil of ignorance leads to the reverse of Rawls's difference principle, this would discredit the plausibility of the device itself (Harris, 1988:90).

A clarifying point is needed here. The difference principle does not *always* yield recommendations at odds with maximizing utility. Rawls suggests that rational egoists choosing behind a veil of ignorance would adopt a 'maximin' strategy (Rawls, 1971:152–3). They would seek to maximize what they would get if they ended up in the minimum, or worst-off, position. In this way he arrives at the difference principle: inequalities in wealth and resources are justifiable only in so far as they operate to the advantage of the worst-off members of society. However, in the veil of ignorance example we are at present considering, there is no way of maximizing the level of the worst-off: no strategy can present the rational egoist with anything better than certain death if he or she loses. So a supporter of the difference principle could, without inconsistency, defer to the strategy of maximizing utility in the present case. Nevertheless, as we have seen, the two principles may on other occasions issue in incompatible recommendations, and if these two principles with their quite different recommendations are derivable from the one device of choice behind a veil of ignorance, Harris argues, this must call into question the device itself.

But there is another possibility here. Perhaps it is not the device itself that should be questioned, but the derivation from it of Rawls's difference principle. There have long been grounds for thinking that in *A Theory of Justice* Rawls 'cooked the books' in order to derive from his hypothetical device the principles that he believed agreed with our considered moral judgments about justice (see Barry, 1973: ch. 9). In his own later work, Rawls has effectively conceded this point, for he has shifted away from defending the two principles of justice in terms of their derivation from a choice made by rational egoists under conditions of ignorance, and instead has focused on the 'fundamental ideas viewed as latent in the public political culture of a democratic society' (Rawls, 1988:252). If it is right that rational egoists behind a veil of ignorance would opt for a QALY-based method of allocating health care, and if this is incompatible with the principles of justice Rawls claims to have derived from the hypothetical choices of rational egoists, then perhaps this discredits Rawls's derivation of the two principles of justice rather than the device of hypothetical choice itself.

Rational Choice and Likelihood

Equal Chances and Unequal Gains

Harris argues that a rational egoist would only choose to allocate life-saving treatment in accordance with the QALY method if he or she had a better than 50/50 chance of receiving that treatment, which is not the case in our example. If there was only a 50/50 chance, the rational egoist would, according to Harris, allocate randomly, and disregard any information about how intensely a person desires to go on living: 'A rational egoist would surely only give preference to saving the life of the person with the highest interest in continued existence, when he is also *most likely to be that person*. If he has no better than a 50/50 chance of being that person, it cannot be in his interest to prioritise the life of such a person because he cannot know that he won't in fact be worsening his own chances; the same goes of course for non life-saving gains' (Harris, 1995:153).

But Harris has made an elementary error here. Whether treatment is offered on the basis of QALYs or randomly, since it is only offered to one person, there is a 50 per cent chance of being the person who receives no treatment and dies. Since this is common to both methods of allocation, the rational egoist could disregard it. But similarly, on both methods there is a 50 per cent chance of being the person whose life is saved. So, on the one hand, what the rational egoist is offered if treatment is allocated according to the QALY method is a 50 per cent chance of getting a comparatively big QALY gain: for example, turning out to be Zach, and having life-saving treatment when his prospects are for a long life of good quality. On the other hand, what the rational egoist is offered if treatment is allocated randomly is a 25 per cent chance of the same big utility gain and a 25 per cent chance of a smaller utility gain: for example, turning out to be Arne, and having life-saving treatment when his quality of life will be poor. Recall that with the heart transplant Arne will have 20 QALYs and Zach 38. Thus the expected gain of the rational egoist if treatment is allocated according to the cost-per-QALY decision rule, but before the veil is lifted, is 50 per cent of 38 QALYs, that is, 19 QALYs. On the other hand, the expected gain of the rational egoist if treatment is allocated randomly is 25 per cent of 38 QALYs + 25 per cent of 20 QALYs, that is, 14.5 QALYs. So, contrary to what Harris maintains, a rational egoist could consistently distinguish between two options, each of which offered the same chances of success and failure, if what he or she stood to gain was different in each case. It is not the case that a 'rational egoist would surely only give preference to saving the life of the person with the highest interest in continued existence, when he is also *most likely to be that person*'.

Of course, this assumes that it makes sense to talk about some people's interest in continued life being low while that of others is high, and this is something that Harris rejects (ibid.:151). He concedes that it makes sense for an individual, when comparing alternative futures, to prefer one to another: it makes sense to say that an individual has a greater interest in continued life under one set of conditions compared with another. But Harris rejects the idea that it makes sense when comparing the alternative futures of different people. However, this scepticism seems unwarranted. Although it is not possible to compare directly one person's interest in living with another's, it does not follow that interpersonal comparisons of quality of life are meaningless. Imagine there has been a car accident, as a result of which several people have sustained similar injuries and are in pain, but we have enough painkiller for only one person. Assume also that anything less than a full dose is ineffective. In this situation we do the best we can to make a judgment about which individual is in the most pain (on the assumption that helping this person first will do the most good) based on the criteria of pain severity with which we are all familiar: the nature of the injuries, how bad they say their pain is, their other responses to those injuries, and so on. If one person's pain rated high on these indicators and the other's low, and other things were equal, we would *not* toss a coin. Even if we might be mistaken, the most responsible thing to do would be to rely on these admittedly imperfect indicators, especially if the gap is large, and give the painkiller to the person we believe is in most pain (if the severity of the pain does not mean that the painkiller would be ineffective).

It is also important to distinguish clearly between the interests of the rational egoist who must choose from behind a veil of ignorance, and the interests of the individual who is saved once the veil is lifted. A rational egoist behind a veil of ignorance will have a greater interest in living a life of good quality rather than in living a life of poor quality. But, once the veil is lifted, *whichever individual is saved* may express the same interest in life as other individuals, and through all his or her actions indicate the same interest. But resource allocation decisions must be made before individuals know which treatments they may need, if those decisions are to be made impartially. And the attraction of the veil of ignorance is that it facilitates impartial choices; it requires us to compare and evaluate our interest in continuing to live without a prior commitment to some particular alternative. Without such a commitment a rational egoist may well state or reveal that they have a greater interest in living in one health state (for example, being able to move around freely) rather than another (for example, being confined to a wheelchair). It is for this reason that we can say that an 'interest in continued life' in one health state is greater than in another: individuals rank their interest in health states in this way when choice is necessary, and when their choice is impartial. But, to repeat, once the veil is lifted, a person with a poor quality of life may express the same, or even a greater, desire to live than a person with a comparatively good quality of life.

Cohen reports a study which found that patients with previous intensive care unit experience tend to exhibit 'extreme willingness to undergo intensive care regardless of their age, functional status, perceived quality of life, hypothetical life expectancy, or the nature of their previous intensive care unit experience' (Cohen, 1996:269). These patients wanted to prolong their lives regardless of the quality, so long as it was not devastatingly bad. But we should not be too hasty in inferring from this that 'there is reason to be somewhat sceptical about the significance of the quality of life component in valuing life' or that 'the importance of quality of life improvements compared to extending survival duration may be somewhat exaggerated by the researchers' (ibid.). It is not inconsistent for a disabled person to value their life and intensely want to go on living, and yet at the same time wish they did not have their disability. It is not inconsistent to prefer a life of good quality to a life of poor quality, and yet prefer to live rather than die whether disabled or not. So choosing survival even when facing a life of disability does not call into question 'the significance of the quality of life component in valuing life'. Quality of life remains important. People without a vested interest – people asked to choose impartially (from behind a veil of ignorance) – will, if they are rational and well informed, prefer a life of good quality to a life of poor quality. So, even though QALYs give preference to those with a higher quality of life (other things being equal) and even though people want to prolong their lives regardless of the quality (unless it is extremely bad), rational egoists would still choose to allocate in accordance with QALYs: they would do this because they are choosing from behind a veil of ignorance, and therefore would give preference to living a life of good quality. Being in ignorance of their own position, they would choose to maximize QALYs.

'Eligibility' for Survival

A second argument Harris presents against allocation on the basis of QALYs, and in favour of random allocation, also appeals to the chances facing the rational egoist behind a veil of ignorance. For this argument, rather than assuming there is a 50 per cent chance of being Arne and a 50 per cent chance of being Zach, Harris assumes that 50 per cent of the population will receive treatment and survive, whereas the other 50 per cent will receive no treatment and die. The rational egoist must then choose between the QALY method of allocation, which would ensure treatment for that 50 per cent of the population with the highest QALY scores, and the random method, which would select a random 50 per cent of the population for treatment. Of course, the rational egoist does not know whether he or she has a high or a low QALY score:

> If QALYs are used as the allocation procedure, only 50% of the population will be eligible for survival. If random methods are used 100% will be eligible. In each case 50% will survive. Would the rational egoist opt for a method where only 50% of the population have a chance of survival and he has no reason to suppose he will be in that privileged 50%, rather than a method where 100% have a chance and he knows he will be one of those with a chance because all have a chance? (Harris, 1996:211)

Only 50 per cent of the population will be 'eligible' for survival if the QALY method is used in the sense that only 50 per cent of the population have a sufficiently high QALY score to survive. Even prior to the veil being lifted, 50 per cent of the population are debarred in this sense, though the rational egoist does not know whether he or she belongs to this group or not. By contrast, 100 per cent of the population will be 'eligible' if the random method is used, in the sense that any individual might get lucky when the veil is lifted, even if they have a low QALY score. In brief, with the random method the rational egoist has a 100 per cent chance of a 50 per cent chance of survival, despite his or her QALY score, whereas with the QALY method he or she has only a 50 per cent chance of survival, since only 50 per cent of the population have a QALY score high enough. Who would not prefer a 100 per cent chance to a 50 per cent chance?

But it is not difficult to spot the error Harris has made here. The apparent advantage of the random method arises from an inconsistency in the meaning of 'eligible' in the passage cited, and an implied numerical error in the calculation of the probability of survival arising from this. If random methods are used it is true that 100 per cent will be 'eligible', but 'eligibility' here implies the right to a 50 per cent chance of survival. If the QALY method is used 50 per cent will be 'eligible', but here 'eligibility' implies a guarantee of survival. The overall probability of survival, correctly calculated by the rational egoist, will be identical if the misleading use of the term 'eligibility' is clarified. There is no advantage in having a 100 per cent chance of being 'eligible' for survival prior to the lifting of the veil if there is still only a 50 per cent chance of surviving once the veil is lifted. A 100 per cent chance of a 50 per cent chance is still only a 50 per cent chance. With the random method, the event that determines the fate of the rational egoist occurs after the veil is lifted: a coin is tossed, for example, and he or she either gets the life-saving treatment or does not. With the QALY method, the event or events determining the fate of the rational egoist (that is, all of the events that have shaped his or her QALY score) have already occurred before the deliberations begin. This is why Harris says that only 50 per cent of the population are eligible for survival on the QALY method. But this should make no difference to the rational egoist. The rational egoist knows neither his or her QALY score nor what the result of the coin toss will be; he or she only knows that there is a 50 per cent chance of having a low QALY score and (a 100 per cent chance of) a 50 per cent chance of losing the coin toss. The rational egoist will therefore look at which system offers the greatest rewards if he or she *does* win.

This point can be made by means of a simple example. Imagine that you must choose under which of two cups a pea is hidden, and that you have the choice of playing one of two games. With *game 1* the pea is already hidden under one of the cups, but you do not know which one. With *game 2* the pea will be deposited under one of the two cups by a totally arbitrary procedure after you make your selection (say, by pointing to a cup). Would you prefer to play one game to the other? Clearly, there is no rational ground on which to prefer one to the other. Nor would it make any difference if you were given the following information. The cup under which the pea is placed in *game 1* is determined by your height (or some other genetically determined characteristic): if you are over a certain height the pea will be placed in one particular cup (though you do not know which one) and if you are below that height it will be placed in the other. It would seem that one game is still as good as the other, because both offer a 50 per cent chance of winning and a 50 per cent chance of losing. By contrast, Harris would maintain that a rational egoist would prefer to play *game 2*. With *game 1*, he would argue, there is only a 50 per cent chance of winning, because 50 per cent of the population are antecedently precluded from winning by virtue of their height. But with *game 2* there is a 100 per cent chance of being 'eligible' to win, because everyone has a chance of picking the right cup in *game 2* regardless of their height. The fallacy in this reasoning should be obvious: there is no difference between having a 50 per cent chance of winning and having a 100 per cent chance of a 50 per cent chance of winning. It is totally irrelevant from the point of view of the person making the choice that the pea is already deposited under one of the cups in *game 1*, and that this depends on his or her height. This only means that there is no difference between being 'eligible' to win and actually winning in *game 1*. So *game 1* offers a 50 per cent chance of winning (which is equivalent to being 'eligible' to win), whereas there is a 100 per cent chance of a 50 per cent chance of winning in *game 2*. But this is an empty distinction: from the point of view of the person making the decision, both games still offer a 50 per cent chance of winning and a 50 per cent chance of losing, and that is all that is relevant.

Imagine now that you are told that the pea in *game 1* is made of gold and is worth $1000, whereas the pea in *game 2* is made of silver and is worth $500. In both games, the winner gets to keep the pea. Would you prefer one game to the other now? If you are rational and self-interested, you would. If your chances of winning and losing are the same in both games (and the consequences of losing are the same) you would opt for the game which offers the greatest benefits if you *do* win. By contrast, Harris would maintain that you would only opt for the game offering the greater benefit if you had a greater chance of winning: 'A rational egoist would surely only give preference to saving the life of the person with the highest interest in continued existence, when he is also *most likely to be that person*.' This is clearly false: it is better to play *game 1* than *game 2* if the former offers the more valuable prize.

Identity Behind the Veil

Harris also sees relevance in the fact that the veil of ignorance 'precedes' identity, but does not 'conceal' it (Harris, 1996:213). In other words, Harris thinks about the rational egoist behind the veil of ignorance as an actual person, with fixed characteristics beyond being merely rational and self-interested; in particular, they either have a high or a low QALY score. Harris believes this is relevant because it makes a difference to the chances facing the rational egoist. If the rational egoist is a real person (if the veil *conceals* his or her identity but does not *precede* it) – that is, if he or she has a determinate QALY score – then they only have a 50 per cent chance of being 'eligible' to survive. Whereas on the random method they have a 100 per cent chance of being 'eligible' to survive, despite their QALY score. But, as we have seen, this is not relevant. It makes no difference that 50 per cent of the population playing *game 1* is 'ineligible' to win because they have a 50 per cent chance of being too tall (or too short). This only means that being 'eligible' to win and winning are the same in *game 1*. A rational egoist would still reason, correctly, that having a 50 per cent chance of winning is no worse than having a 100 per cent chance of a 50 per cent chance of winning. Indeed, knowing that the potential reward is bigger in *game 1*, the rational egoist will prefer it to *game 2* with its random method of allocation.

Harris also thinks it is a mistake to treat the rational egoist as a candidate in a lottery in which the draw will take place at or after the lifting of the veil. This assumes, incorrectly according to Harris, that the rational egoist has a certain chance of winning or losing. However, unless identity occurs after the lifting of the veil, this is not the situation. Rather the lottery was run a long time ago and people are born with tickets that are already winning or losing tickets – they have no chance of either winning or losing with the tickets they possess because they already have won or lost. (Ibid.)

But it is irrelevant that 'the lottery was run a long time ago'. It is irrelevant that the cup under which the pea is placed in *game 1* is determined by your height, which is determined by your genes – that is, something set 'a long time ago'. It is true that, if you choose to play *game 1*, you are 'born with a ticket that is already winning or losing', in the sense that the pea has been placed under a particular cup prior to your choice. This means that you only win if you are 'eligible' to win; in other words, being 'eligible' to win and winning are the same thing. But it is not true that you 'have no chance of either winning or losing with the ticket [you] possess because [you] already have won or lost'. You still have a 50 per cent chance of winning and a 50 per cent chance of losing, depending on which cup you choose. Similarly, in Harris's example, as a rational egoist you have a 50 per cent chance of having a high QALY score, and a 50 per cent chance of having a low QALY score: you have these chances because you are behind a veil of ignorance and do not know your own health status.

The veil of ignorance forces impartial choices by preventing people knowing whether they will be advantaged or disadvantaged by a proposed social arrangement. And, if the previous arguments are sound, this test suggests that it would be rational to choose a system that gives preference to saving life when it is most in the interests of the person whose life is saved. In other words, if Rawls's veil of ignorance test leads to fairness, it is not unfair to give a lower priority to saving the lives of those with incurable conditions that significantly reduce their quality of life or life expectancy, if our resources are limited and we cannot save every life that could be saved by some form of health care. It would seem, then, that what double jeopardy there is in the QALY approach does not make it unfair, or warrant its rejection.

Notes

1   In rejecting the Oregon plan for rationing health care, the United States Secretary for Health and Human Services also used a form of the 'double jeopardy' argument. (See Louis Sullivan, Press Release, 3 August 1992, Health and Human Services Press Office, cited in Daniels (1993:227.)

2   See McTurk (1994:27): 'interpersonal comparisons of utility ... are a part of everyday life, albeit unformalised ... . If QALYs are to be rejected because they

attempt this task, then so are methods of allocation that are based on comparisons of need, including equal access for equal need. We should be seeking ways of doing this beter, not rejecting QALYs because they do it imperfectly.' See also Rawls (1971:91): 'skepticism about interpersonal comparisons is often based on questionable views: for example, that the intensity of pleasure or of the enjoyment which indicates well-being is the intensity of pure sensation; and that while the intensity of such sensations can be experienced and known by the subject, it is impossible for others to know it or to infer it with reasonable certainty. Both these contentions seem wrong. Indeed, the second is simply part of a skepticism about the existence of other minds, unless it is shown why judgements of well-being present special problems which cannot be overcome.'

6 Public Opinion

If we were to base the allocation of health care resources solely on the QALY approach, we would be assuming, as we have seen, that the distribution of QALYs among the population is unimportant. We might refer to this as the assumption of *distributive neutrality*. But we have also seen that this assumption has been challenged. One way of addressing this challenge, while retaining an important role for the QALY, is by recognizing that QALYs measure only health-related quality of life and acknowledging that there are other factors that make up our overall quality of life. These other factors will, of course, be very varied. They will include our personal relationships, our satisfaction with our work and our leisure opportunities. They may also include the knowledge that we are living in a certain kind of society. For example, in deciding on the allocation of health care resources, we may take into account not only the maximization of QALYs, but also the extent to which we are taking good care of the least fortunate members of our society.

Since we are now entering the realm of community values, it is interesting to ask what stance the general public takes on this issue. Do most people agree, when the issue is explained to them in a manner that they can understand, that health care resources should be allocated solely according to the principle of maximizing QALYs, assuming that the value assigned to a QALY is the same no matter who receives it? What do they think about the implications of this assumption? Knowing the views of the general public on this matter is important. Even those who think that allocation decisions should be made by experts, or by the democratically elected representatives of the community in parliament, will hardly be able to deny that those experts or representatives should be aware of what the community's views are. It is hard to think of promoting the welfare of the community without some knowledge of the community's wishes.

As Olsen notes (1994), the assumption of distributive neutrality has implications along two different lines. The first is that the value of a QALY is assumed to be independent of the personal character-istics of the recipient. Williams (1981) acknowledged that this assumption is questionable, and various surveys have confirmed this. Wright (1986) found that people considered it more important to maintain the health of children and parents of young children than that of other age groups. The view that children and young adults – particularly those with dependent children – should have some pri-ority over elderly people also seems to have considerable public support in Wales, Sweden and Holland (see Charny *et al.*, 1989; Braakenhielm, 1990; Bjork and Rosen, 1993; Busschbach *et al.*, 1993), but less so in Norway (see the Norwegian Commission on Prioritising in Health Care, 1987; Nord, 1993b). The Welsh and Swedish studies also showed a tendency for people to extend priority to patients with a 'healthy' lifestyle over patients with an 'unhealthy' lifestyle.

The second implication of distributive neutrality is that the value of each QALY is the same irrespective of how many QALYs a person receives. This has the further implication that, for equally ill patients, those who will benefit more from treatment, in terms of either qual-ity or quantity of life received, should have priority over those who will benefit less. This conflicts with a common view – the official view in Norway, for example (see the Norwegian Commission on Prioritising in Health Care, 1987) – that everybody has a right to realize his or her *potential* for improvement, be this large or small. It also runs counter to a study by Nord (1993a) which suggests that people wish to extend equal priority to groups who are equally ill so long as care will provide all of them with a substantial increase in quality of life. Similarly, in the study by Olsen (1994), subjects typi-cally thought that 10 years of benefit gained by 100 people was equivalent in social value to 20 years of benefit received by 80 peo-ple. While this might reflect time preference,[1] it could also reflect equity preferences; that is, 'diminishing social valuation of a person's succeeding years with improved health' (ibid.:40). This would imply that, when QALY gains are concentrated among few people, they are less valued than when they are more widely distributed.

In short, there is some evidence to suggest that the general public does not want to see health care resources allocated solely on the basis that QALYs should be maximized. In the next section, we present further evidence of this, based on a survey we recently carried out in Australia.

An Australian Survey

In 1994, we investigated whether members of the Australian public agree with the economic goal of maximizing QALYs, or whether in

Australia, too, there is a rejection of the assumption of distributive neutrality that this would imply. We began by identifying four key distributional implications of the QALY maximization approach:

1   In the case of life-saving or enduring life-improving interventions, young patients will, other things being equal, have priority over older patients;
2   if patients are suffering equally, those with the greater potential for improvement have priority over those with a lesser potential for improvement;
3   patients with family responsibilities will not be treated differently from patients without such responsibilities; and
4   patients with illnesses that result from their own past unhealthy lifestyles will receive the same treatment as patients who bear no responsibility for their own ill health.

Of these implications, the first two follow directly from the idea of maximizing the number of quality-adjusted life years gained by treatment, whereas the last two are implied by the fact that, at least on standard interpretations of the QALY procedure, we take into account only future health-related benefits to the patient.

Not everyone agrees with these four propositions. Some doctors, for example, believe that those responsible for their ill health should have low priority in treatment, while others think that medical decision making should, at least sometimes, focus not only on the patient, but also on the effect that a medical decision has on the family. Those who disagree with one or more of the above four propositions would also disagree with present understandings of the QALY maximization approach, and with the assumed goal of contemporary health care economics.

This was confirmed by our survey (Nord *et al.*, 1995a). We constructed a self-administered questionnaire, which was distributed to a total of 2000 households. The response rate was 28 per cent and, not surprisingly, those responding were, compared with the Australian population as a whole, significantly more likely to have a tertiary qualification. They were also slightly more likely to speak English at home, to be female, and not to smoke.[2] The questionnaire began with the following preamble:

> In our society there is not enough money to give all patients all the health care they want. There is also a shortage of donor organs for patients in need of organ transplantations. In practice, this means that some patients get treated more quickly than others. It can also mean that some patients receive certain kinds of expensive treatment while others do not. In both cases we may say that some patients are given *priority* over others.

On what basis should priority be given? This is the question that we are asking you to consider in this study.

The recipients of the questionnaire were faced with the following six implications of the assumption of distributive neutrality:

1   (AGE/LIFE): Among people with life-threatening illnesses, younger patients should have some priority over older patients (since, all else equal, more QALYs will be gained).
2   (AGE/QoL): For medical care that improves quality of life permanently, young people should have some priority over elderly people (since, all else equal, more QALYs will be gained).
3   (NEWBORN): If a young child and a newborn infant both need the same organ transplant and there is only one organ available, the newborn infant should have priority (since, assuming equal chances of success, more QALYs will be gained).
4   (POTENTIAL): Among patients who are suffering equally, some priority should be given to those who have the greatest potential for improvement (since, all else equal, more QALYs will be gained).
5   (PARENTS): For the same severity of illness, people without children should have the same priority as people with children (since, all else equal, the number of QALYs gained will be the same).
6   (SMOKERS): Smokers and non-smokers should have equal priority with respect to treatment for heart disease and lung cancer (assuming that the expected number of QALYs gained is the same).

The first four of these propositions are implications of the view that QALYs are equally valued by society irrespective of the number of QALYs each person receives. Propositions 5 and 6 are implications of the view that the personal characteristics of the recipients are irrelevant to the value placed on QALYs by society. Table 6.1 shows the distribution of choices on the six different issues as well as the distributions of respondents by how difficult they found the various choices.

The *first question* asked respondents to choose between options about life-saving treatments. The questionnaire presented the following options:

1   Among people with life-threatening illnesses, younger patients should have some priority over older patients.
2   People should have the same priority with respect to life-saving treatment, unless they are very old.
3   People should have the same priority with respect to life-saving treatment, no matter what their age is.

Table 6.1 Response to each issue and difficulty of choice (%)

Issue	Option	Percentage choosing each option	Difficulty of choice		
			Very difficult (%)	Slightly difficult (%)	Not difficult (%)
AGE/LIFE	Favour young	17.6	28.0	35.5	36.6
	Against very old	40.5	26.2	48.6	25.2
	Equal priority	41.9	16.7	24.0	59.3
AGE/QoL	Favour young	21.5	36.0	35.1	28.8
	Favour old	2.9	13.3	46.7	40.0
	Equal priority	75.6	15.3	23.8	60.9
NEWBORN	Favour young child	44.2	40.1	30.4	29.5
	Favour newborn	1.2	66.7	16.7	16.7
	Equal priority	54.7	43.1	16.0	40.9
POTENTIAL	Favour most helped	52.8	29.4	30.9	39.7
	Equal priority	47.2	22.2	30.0	47.7
PARENTS	Favour parents	33.4	30.0	34.7	35.3
	Equal priority	66.6	10.0	14.7	75.2
SMOKERS	Favour non-smokers	59.5	15.2	18.8	66.0
	Equal priority	40.5	18.4	22.8	58.7

Source: Nord *et al.* (1995a).

Of respondents, 41.9 per cent chose option 3 (equal priority), that is, they were not prepared to discriminate on the basis of age, compared to 17.6 per cent who gave some priority to younger patients (option 1); 40.5 per cent chose not to discriminate, unless the patients were very old (option 2). 41.5 per cent of respondents did not find it difficult to reach their decision, compared to 22.5 per cent who found it a very difficult choice. However, those choosing to discriminate on the basis of age expressed greater difficulty making their choice than did those opting for equal priority (see Table 6.1).

Given that the question asked about life-saving treatments, the assumptions of health benefit maximization and distributive neutrality in a system of distribution based purely on counting QALYs should lead to a preference for the treatment going to the young since, other things being equal, they will have longer to live, and so more QALYs will be gained. The answers reveal, however, that a preference for treatment going to the young is not widely held in the Australian community. Interestingly, those older than 65 were more prepared to discriminate on the basis of age, with only 31.8 per cent opting for equal priority irrespective of age compared to 45.2 per cent of those under 65 who chose this option.

The *second question* posed a choice about treatments that made a permanent improvement in quality of life. The options were as follows:

1   For medical care that improves quality of life permanently, young people should have some priority over elderly people.
2   For medical care that improves quality of life permanently, elderly people should have some priority over young people.
3   People should have the same priority with respect to medical care that improves quality of life permanently, no matter what their age is.

As with life-saving treatments, the pursuit of health benefit maximization based solely on distributive neutrality would favour permanent quality of life improvements going to those who will benefit from them for the longest time. But this view again received only weak support. Only 21.5 per cent favoured giving priority to the young (option 1) while 75.6 per cent selected the equal priority view (option 3). Most of the latter group said they made the choice without difficulty (see Table 6.1).

We initially expected more responses favouring the young in the life-saving context (question 1) than in the quality of life improvement context (question 2). In fact, the difference is small and in the opposite direction. This could be due to the difference between the second options in the two questions. However, consistent with our expectations, less difficulty of choice was reported among respondents favouring the young with respect to life-saving treatments than among respondents favouring the young when treatments that improved quality of life were considered (see Table 6.1).

The *third question* was as follows:

Consider a situation in which a young child and a newborn infant both need the same organ transplant. There is only one organ available. Which of the following do you agree with?

1   The young child should have the organ.
2   The newborn infant should have the organ.
3   No preference.

Of all the issues considered, people found it hardest to reach a decision on this one, with 52 per cent saying that their choice had been very difficult to make. The respondents were asked to consider 'all else equal'. This was meant to include equality in the chance of a successful operation. Given this assumption, the view that the newborn infant should have the organ would fit best with the health benefit maximization assumption underlying a purely QALY-based allocation procedure. However, only 1.2 per cent of the respondents chose this view; 54.7 per cent indicated that there should be no preference between the two requiring the organ, and many of the respondents explicitly commented that the decision should be made on a first come, first serve basis; 44.2 per cent said that the young child should be favoured. Prima facie, these results would once again seem to contradict the assumptions of health benefit maximization and distributive neutrality.

On the other hand, according to the written comments that were given on this issue, a considerable number who expressed no preference would give priority to the one with the better expected outcome. This does accord with pure health benefit maximization. Moreover, the most common reason for opting for the young child was that the respondents assumed that the young child had a better chance of a successful operation. As noted above, it was not intended that the subjects make this assumption, but since it was in fact made, their preference for the young child must be seen as reflecting a benefit-maximizing attitude rather than as a rejection of it.

Other comments suggest that the young child was considered to be 'more of a person', with a greater capacity to experience pain and grief if denied life-saving care. Also the loss of the young child, being older, was thought to be more acutely felt by parents and others than the loss of the newborn infant who has not had the opportunity to touch as many lives. Hence the grief caused by the loss of a young child would be greater. But explanations of these two kinds were notably less common than those referring to chances of success.

There were differences in the choice of options depending on the characteristics of the respondents, but only education had a significant effect on choice. Those with tertiary education were more likely to opt for equal priority than those with a lower level of education.

On balance, the results from this question reveal fairly strong concerns about the goal of maximizing benefits alone. Nevertheless, comments about the young child being more of a person suggest that the assumption of distributive neutrality may be rejected by quite a few subjects.

The *fourth question* examined support for health benefit maximization and distributive neutrality concerning the question whether those who will be helped most by a given treatment should have priority over those for whom the benefit will be less. The options were presented as follows:

1   Among patients who are suffering equally, some priority should be given to those who will be helped most from treatment.
2   Among patients who are suffering equally, those who can become a little better should have the same priority as those who can become much better.

There was an even balance between those giving some priority to patients who will be helped most (52.8 per cent) and those favouring equality (47.2 per cent). There was a slight tendency for the former to find their choice more difficult to make (see Table 6.1). Men were more likely than women to give some priority to patients who will be helped most, and the same applies to those in paid (full-time or part-time) work, when compared with respondents not so employed.

The bearing of these data on the question of support for allocation based solely on health benefit maximization and distributive neutrality is not clear. But it is worth pointing out some elements in the formulations that were used. Option 1 uses the expression 'some priority', which in itself is an expression of weak preference. On the other hand, option 2 compared those who can become only 'a little better' with those who can become 'much better'. This description of a quite large difference in outcome did not make option 2 an obvious choice. Nonetheless, some 47 per cent chose it. In light of this, it is reasonable to conclude that the responses to this question suggest only weak support from the Australian public for the allocation of health care resources entirely on the basis of assumptions of health benefit maximization and distributive neutrality.

As we have noted (p. 41), the pure QALY procedure has been criticized for failing to include the benefits of treatment to anyone other than the patients themselves. In particular, it has been argued that the positive effects on people who are dependent on the patients should be incorporated in the assessment of health programmes. This issue was addressed in the *fifth question*. Respondents were offered the following choices:

1   Parents with dependent children should have some priority over other adults.
2   For the same illness, people without children should have the same priority as people with children.

Only 33.4 per cent were prepared to favour parents with dependent children (option 1), the remainder giving equal priority to adults with dependents and those without. Respondents in the latter group also reported having made their choices with greater ease than the former group (see Table 6.1). There is therefore strong support for the assumption of distributive neutrality on this particular issue.

The *final question* explored attitudes to illnesses related to lifestyle. It used cigarette smoking as an example and read as follows:

Many people enjoy cigarette smoking. But cigarette smoking is also a cause of heart disease and lung cancer. Which of the following do you agree with?

1   If there is not enough money to treat everybody with heart disease or lung cancer, non-smokers should have some priority over smokers.
2   Smokers should have the same priority with respect to treatment for heart disease and lung cancer as everybody else.

Of the respondents, 59.5 per cent believed that some priority should be exercised in favour of non-smokers, the remainder opting not to discriminate, and respondents found this the easiest of the six issues on which to reach a decision, with 63.1 per cent saying that their choice had not been difficult to make. These results would lend some support to allocating health care resources solely on the basis of health benefit maximization and distributive neutrality, if people who preferred option 1 did so because they thought outcomes tend to be better in non-smokers than in smokers. However, while some respondents did refer to this aspect in their comments, the great majority blamed smokers for having behaved so as to bring about their own illnesses. These explanations reflect the influence of moral attitudes that are a departure from the assumption of distributive neutrality.

As might be expected, smokers were more likely to give equal priority to smokers and non-smokers, with 69 per cent opting for equality compared to only 35.5 per cent of respondents who were non-smokers. Even so, it is interesting that 31 per cent of smokers were prepared to vote (in effect) against their own interests. The elderly and those with private insurance were more likely to favour treatment for non-smokers.

In summary, the study suggests that the allocation of health care resources purely on a basis that assumes distributive neutrality receives:

1   very little support when health benefits to young people compete with health benefits to the elderly;
2   only moderate support when those who can become a little better compete with those who can become much better;
3   only moderate support when smokers compete with non-smokers;
4   some support when young children compete with newborns; and
5   wide support when parents of dependent children compete with adults without children.

Overall, there is a strong egalitarian tendency – in the sense of 'equal access to health care' rather than in the sense of counting everyone's QALYs equally – in the views of the Australians we surveyed. In particular, a policy based solely on health benefit maximization receives very limited support when the consequence is a loss of access to services for the elderly and for people with a restricted potential for becoming better. The egalitarian view is also apparent in the majority's preference for treating parents and non-parents and newborn and young children equally. It is only when comparing smokers with non-smokers that a clear deviation from egalitarianism is observed. These conclusions are strengthened by the results in Table 6.1 suggesting that respondents generally had less difficulty in selecting the 'egalitarian' option than in supporting a discriminating view (again with the exception of the smoking issue). Our findings are also broadly in line with the overseas studies mentioned at the beginning of this chapter.

Taken together, the survey findings represent a significant challenge to a purely QALY-based approach. They do not render QALYs useless, because they give no reason for thinking that the information provided by QALY analysis should not be taken into account in allocating health care resources. But they do suggest that most people think that QALYs should not be the sole basis for this allocation. This raises the question: what weight should be given to the views of the population on an issue of this kind?

Public Opinion, Ethics and Economic Evaluation

Some economists may claim that public opinion on the ethics of allocating health care resources should not be taken into consideration, because the use of the QALY method is ethically neutral. All the QALY method does, these economists may say, is make rigorous and measurable what we all want, as evidenced by our answers, not to questions about ethical issues of distribution, as asked in the survey just discussed, but to the specific surveys seeking our preferences about health states, as discussed previously in Chapter 2.

The claim that the QALY method is ethically neutral is in keeping with the belief that economics is really a value-free science. On this view, economics is the study of the allocation of finite resources to maximize welfare, and welfare should be understood as the satisfaction of preferences, which in practice economists usually take to be the preferences revealed by consumers making choices in the market-place. Given this, there should be no ethical problems about the economic evaluation of health care. All we have to do is find out what people prefer, as far as their health is concerned, and then distribute our health care resources so as to maximize this. The economic evaluation of health care would then be a scientific enterprise without substantive ethical content.

This defence of disregarding public opinion about the way resources should be distributed, in favour of the exclusive use of QALYs, should be rejected. QALY theorists may indeed construct their scales by finding ingenious ways of asking people which health states they prefer and by how much, but there is a gap between this fact and the claim that the allocation of health care in accordance with QALYs is ethically neutral. The fact that everyone would prefer one state of health to another does not allow us to deduce that we ought to allocate our resources so as to provide everyone with that state of health, strictly in accordance with the principle of maximizing the satisfaction of their health-related preferences. It is possible for people to hold that some are more deserving of better health than others, and to think it right to distribute health care resources on the basis of desert (for example, with less going to those who have been reckless about their health). One can argue against such a view, but to argue against it is to take a substantive ethical stance. Thus there is no 'ethically neutral' solution to the problem of allocating health care resources.

What, then, is the role of public opinion, of the kind revealed by the survey we have just described, in allocating health care resources? There is a straightforwardly pragmatic reason for believing that public opinion does matter: a government that uses an unpopular method of allocating health care resources is likely to face strong opposition, and may well retreat in the face of that opposition. Thus economists who favour QALYs should be concerned that the evidence of our survey, and others mentioned earlier in this chapter, suggests that it will be difficult for some governments to act on the basis of a pure QALY approach. Anyone who is concerned about the consequences of policies – as proponents of QALYs are – will presumably also be concerned about whether or not a recommended policy is likely to be implemented. This suggests that such economists may need to consider a compromise between the method of allocating health care resources that they believe would be best, if it could be implemented, and a less satisfactory approach, so that the final result is a method that the public will be prepared to accept and the government will be able to implement.

Suppose, for example, that in Ruritania health care resources are distributed on a historical basis, with most resources going to long-established health care institutions which have not adjusted to changes in health problems in the population. Thus at present the distribution of resources is extremely inefficient, from a QALY point of view, with large amounts of money going to health care programmes that gain few QALYs for each $1000 spent, and small amounts of money going to programmes that gain many QALYs per $1000 spent. A newly-elected government proposes to reform the allocation of health care resources. Conservatives oppose the reform measure and are seeking to enlist public opinion on their side. Surveys show that public opinion does want to see health care resources used more efficiently, in something like QALY terms, but the public also accords considerable weight to a principle of equality of access to health care. In these circumstances, it would be foolish – and inconsistent with a concern for the consequences of one's actions – for an advocate of QALYs to disregard public opinion. The result may then be that the opportunity for reform is missed, and the existing highly inefficient system of resource allocation continues. It would seem wiser for the advocate of QALYs to support, under these circumstances, an approach that trades some benefits, measured in QALY terms, against a higher degree of equality of access than would be achieved by a pure QALY-based system.

A Role for the Expert Committee

It has become popular for politicians to deal with sensitive ethical issues in health care by seeking the advice of an expert committee or other advisory body. Almost every developed nation has had some such body examine ethical issues arising from new developments such as *in vitro* fertilization, brain death or cloning. The committee may include lay people as representatives of the general public, but it usually also includes a number of experts in relevant fields of science. Such committees can help to 'depoliticize' the issue, offering a government that relies on its advice some kind of shield against public criticism of the course taken.

If a committee were set up to decide ethical issues in the allocation of health care resources, how would its members be selected? Neither patients, doctors nor nurses have any special training or skill that qualifies them to answer the moral question of whether we should spend more money on the health needs of particular groups, such as the young, or parents or non-smokers, or whether everyone's QALYs should be counted equally. But this does not mean that there are no forms of expertise that could lead to better decisions in this area. When we consider the answers given to the questions in our survey, we can easily imagine ways in which the thinking of those surveyed may fail to be as clear, rational or free from bias as it should be.

For example, we have seen (pp. 6–8) that there is more to ethical judgments than just the expression of personal feelings, or of the codes of the societies in which we happen to live. But if we acknowledge that *reason* has a role to play in ethics, we must also acknowledge that some people will be better at it than others. University ethics courses are largely concerned with trying to teach these analytical skills. Those people who are better at thinking about moral issues will, other things being equal, be those with a more highly developed ability to think logically. This entails developing a good nose for distinctions, a sharp eye for fallacies and a general ability to distinguish a good argument from a bad one.[3]

Believing that there is a role for clear thinking in ethics need not include a belief in the existence of objective ethical values, or in the possibility of one true and well-founded normative ethical theory that can, at least in principle, guide practice and settle moral disputes; but it presupposes that moral expertise includes 'a critically examined moral perspective' (Nickel, 1988:144); that is, the capacity to make 'informed moral judgments' (Crosthwaite, 1995:372) on the basis of 'beliefs about values and moral norms which have been critically examined, tested for consistency, and systematized to some degree' (Nickel, 1988:144). While such informed moral judgments must not be confused with 'the truth', they may be the best that is available to us. They will be as sound as the reasoning that supports them.

It is also important to be *well-informed* about any factual matters that are relevant to an ethical issue under consideration. For example, when debating the question of whether embryo experimentation should be allowed, it is vital to know what kind of entity the early human embryo is, whether it can feel pain or experience any other sensation, and so on. Similarly, those with an understanding of economic theory will, other things being equal, be better placed to make an informed judgment about the allocation of resources than those who lack this understanding, for an understanding of economic theory can help one to anticipate and understand the economic consequences of different alternatives. Someone considering whether to extend equal priority to the health care needs of the young and the old may not, out of ignorance, even consider the economic consequences of the decision. (Others, of course, may be aware of the economic consequences of the decision, but for various reasons choose to give them little weight. That is a different matter entirely.) So, for reflection on an ethical issue to be informed, it may be necessary to acquire a certain amount of factual knowledge relevant to the issue under consideration.

In discussing fundamental ethical issues, it can also be useful to have an understanding of *moral theories*, such as utilitarianism, theories of justice, of rights, and so on. This not only involves an understanding of the key concepts and values that underpin the relevant theories, but also includes an awareness of the relevant critiques, including those put forward by, for example, contemporary feminists and post-modernists (Crosthwaite, 1995:365). While it would be a mistake to think that any theory or moral approach could ever simply be trotted out and 'applied' to practical problems, there is little doubt that the various theories present a 'storehouse of sophisticated thinking about how particular judgments may be unified into a larger framework' (Jamieson, 1988:136–7). Those who are not familiar with the work already done in their field are likely to repeat old mistakes.

These traits – the ability to reason well, possession of relevant factual knowledge and knowledge of moral theory, among others – help to explain why some people will be better at thinking about complex ethical issues than others. They give us grounds for thinking that a well-chosen committee, given the time and resources to consider ethical issues in the allocation of health care resources, may come up with better answers than members of the general community who have been presented with a questionnaire and given an hour or two to complete it. Nevertheless, these traits are not sufficient to ensure that the committee makes sound decisions. People who can reason well, and are knowledgeable about both factual matters and moral theory, will often disagree widely on moral issues. In general, it will help if members of the committee come to its deliberations with a set of beliefs broadly reflecting those in the community as a whole. At the same time, the committee should not exclude those who are prepared to challenge views that are widely, but uncritically, accepted in the community.

In advocating the use of an expert committee of this kind, we are not departing from our earlier support for the QALY approach. We are here considering the procedures that a government may adopt in order to reach a solution to the question of how health care resources should be allocated, rather than the question of what that solution should be. To the extent that our earlier arguments for the QALY approach are sound, we would expect that an expert committee of the kind described would find them persuasive, and would make recommendations that reflect this, subject to the point made above about the need for compromise, in order to ensure that the recommendations are translated into action, should there be strongly entrenched contrary views in the wider community.

Some will think that the committee approach is elitist and undemocratic in spirit. They will say that it seeks to take important decisions out of the hands of the public and place them in the hands of self-selected 'experts'. They will argue that, in ethics, there are no experts, and the voice of the people must be heard. In an article published in 1980, Ithiel de Sola Pool, an American sociologist, went so far as to suggest that proposals to set up a national commission to study and identify the basic ethical principles which should underlie the conduct of biomedical and behavioural research were 'better suited to Iran's "Revolutionary Council" than to an American political commission' (de Sola Pool, 1980). But the kind of expertise that we have described above has nothing to do with handing over ethical decisions to committees of learned elderly male clerics. Since 1980, as mentioned previously, there has been widespread acceptance in most democracies of ethical commissions on many different issues, and they have not taken these democracies noticeably closer to the kind of theocratic regime that exists in Iran. One crucial distinction is that in the end, it is the democratically elected government that chooses whether to accept or reject the advice of the committee it has appointed, and that government is answerable to the people for that decision. So while the committee may be able to lead popular opinion, if it loses touch with it altogether, it runs the risk of being ignored by a government fearful of the wrath of the voters.

Notes

1 See Chapter 2, note 7.
2 The questionnaire was mainly distributed in the city of Melbourne, Australia, where the project was based. Five districts of Melbourne were selected, representing different levels of socioeconomic status. In addition, four towns across Australia were included in the data collection to test the representativeness of the main results. Altogether, 2000 questionnaires were distributed, with an overall response rate of 28 per cent; 57 per cent of the respondents were female; the

mean age of respondents was 46; 87 per cent of respondents spoke English as their first language; 49 per cent had received tertiary (university or college) education; 43 per cent were in full-time employment, and 18 per cent were retired. Some 34 per cent had received hospital treatment in the previous two years, 8 per cent said they had a major long-term health problem and 24 per cent said they had a slight long-term health problem; 51 per cent of respondents were privately insured and 16 per cent were smokers. For further details, the reader is referred to the original article: Nord *et al.* (1995a).

3   Beauchamp points out, in particular, the importance of being able to anticipate the unexpected implications of an argument: 'a number of writers – not to mention the United States Supreme Court – have addressed the subject of the nature of "persons" when examining such issues as abortion and fetal rights. Some of these writers seemed unaware that their arguments about persons were so broad that they applied to infants and animals as well as to human fetuses. Their arguments thus provided reasons they had not anticipated for granting to fetuses, and even to animals, the same rights that infants enjoy' (Beauchamp, 1982:14).

7 Conclusion

We have defended the QALY approach, and situated it within a broadly utilitarian framework, and in this sense have defended a particular conception of the good: maximizing quantity and quality of life (or, more broadly, utility). But that does not mean we are arguing for an allocation of health care resources based solely on maximizing QALYs, or that we wish to dismiss the preferences of other members of the community. We are aware that many members of the general public, and many of our colleagues, do not share our view; and that there are other alternative ethical theories, perspectives and judgments which those who hold them believe to be supported by equally good or better reasons than those advanced by us.

However, to the extent that moral theories and judgments are fallible and insecure, none of the disputing parties can claim that they are in possession of the truth. Hence our suggestion, in the preceding chapter, that a carefully selected committee of people with skills in reasoning, knowledge of moral theories, relevant non-moral knowledge, sufficient time and a willingness to challenge conventional views may be the best mechanism for deciding on the allocation of health care resources. Perhaps such a committee would endorse a pure QALY approach, but, equally, some committees of people chosen on this basis may well be persuaded by the arguments of those opposed to the exclusive use of QALYs, and would take into account community values and broader aspects of social utility, including the value of being part of a society that takes extra steps to care for its least fortunate members. We would be very surprised, however, if a committee of the kind we have suggested found that QALYs were of no value at all in allocating health care resources.

If the only validation of an ethical judgment lies in the reasoning that supports it, we stand the best chance of getting things right if we test the adequacy of that reasoning in open and informed debate, not only among moral philosophers and economists but among as wide a range of people as possible. The present book may be seen as an illustration of that methodology. We have subjected the QALY approach to critical appraisal and have provided what we regard as the best reasons and arguments for the conclusions we support, on the one hand, and those that we reject, on the other. While we believe that we have good reasons on our side, we stand to be corrected. Only time and continued informed and open debate can tell. We like to see this book as a contribution to that process.

Bibliography

Abel-Smith, B. (1985), 'Global perspective on health service financing', *Social Science and Medicine*, **21**, 957–63.

Aday, L.A., R. Andersen and G.V. Fleming (1980), *Health Care in the U.S.: Equitable for Whom?*, Beverly Hills: Sage Press.

Aristotle (1962), *The Politics*, trans. T.A. Sinclair, Harmondsworth: Penguin Books.

Baron, Jonathan (1993), *Morality and Rational Choice*, Dordrecht: Kluwer Academic Publishers.

Barry, Brian (1973), *The Liberal Theory of Justice*, Oxford: Clarendon Press.

Battin, Margaret P. (1987), 'Age Rationing and the Just Distribution of Health Care: Is There a Duty To Die?', *Ethics*, **97** (2), 317–40.

Beauchamp, Tom L. (1982), 'What Philosophers Can Offer', *The Hastings Center Report*, **12** (3), 13–14.

Beauchamp, Tom L. and James F. Childress (1994), *Principles of Biomedical Ethics*, 4th edn, Oxford: Oxford University Press.

Bentham, Jeremy (1973), *An Introduction to the Principles of Morals and Legislation*, New York: Anchor Press/Doubleday.

Bjork, S. and P. Rosen (1993), 'Prioritising in health care. An empirical study of the views of health care politicians on resource allocation', Institute of Health Economics working paper 1993: 1, Lund.

Bleichrodt, H. (1995), 'QALYs and HYEs: Under what conditions are they equivalent?', *Journal of Health Economics*, **14** (1), 17–39.

Bowling, A. (1995), *Measuring Disease*, Buckingham/Philadelphia: Open University Press.

Bowman, Jan (1991), *Consultation: An Appraisal of Community Perspectives*, background discussion paper prepared by the National Health and Medical Research Council Secretariat, Canberra, Australia.

Boyle, M., W. Furlong and G. Torrance (1995), 'Reliability of the Health Utilities Index – Mark III used in the 1991 cycle 6 Canadian general social survey health questionnaire', *Quality of Life Research*, **4**, 249–57.

Braakenhielm, C.R. (1990), 'Vaard paa lika vilkaar' ('Health care on equal terms'), in J. Caltorp and C.R. Braakenhielm (eds), *Vaardens pris (The price of care)*, Stockholm: Verbum forlag.

Brandt, Richard B. (1959), *Ethical Theory*, Englewood Cliffs, NJ: Prentice-Hall.

Brazier, J., N. Jones and P. Kind (1993), 'Testing the validity of the EuroQoL and comparing it with the SF-36 health survey questionnaire', *Quality of Life Research*, **2**, 169–80.

Brooks, Richard G. (1991), *Health Status and Quality of Life Measurement: Issues and Developments*, Lund: The Swedish Institute for Health Economics.

Brooks, Richard G. (1995), *Health Status Measurement: A Perspective on Change: Issues in Health Care*, London: Macmillan.

Broom, John (1985), 'The Economic Value of Life', *Economica*, **52**, 281–94.

Broom, John (1988), 'Good, Fairness and QALYs', in J.M. Bell and Susan Mendus (eds), *Philosophy and Medical Welfare*, Cambridge: Cambridge University Press.

Buchanan, A. (1989), 'Health-Care Delivery and Resource Allocation', in R.M. Veatch (ed.), *Medical Ethics*, Boston: Jones and Bartlett.

Buchanan, C.L. and Elizabeth W. Prior (1985), 'Freedom vs. Equality: The Distribution of Medical Care', in C.L. Buchanan and E.W. Prior (eds), *Medical Care and Markets: Conflicts Between Efficiency and Justice*, Sydney: George Allen & Unwin.

Busschbach, J.J.V., D.J. Hessing and F.T. de Charro (1993), 'The utility of health at different stages in life: A quantitative approach', *Social Science and Medicine*, **37**, 153–8.

Cairns, John (1991), 'Health, Wealth and Time Preference', Health Economics Research Unit, discussion paper no. 07, University of Aberdeen.

Cairns, John (1992), 'Discounting and Health Benefits: Another Perspective', *Health Economics*, **1** (1), 76–9.

Callahan, Daniel (1987), *Setting Limits: Medical Goals in an Aging Society*, New York: Simon & Schuster.

Callahan, Daniel (1991), *What Kind of Life – The Limits of Medical Progress*, New York: Touchstone.

Campbell, Alastair V. and Grant Gillett (1993), *Ethical Issues in Defining Core Services*, discussion papers prepared for The National Advisory Committee on Core Health and Disability Support Services, Wellington, New Zealand.

Campbell, Tom (1988), *Justice*, London: Macmillan.

Carr-Hill, Roy A. (1989), 'Background Material for the Workshop on QALYs: Assumptions of the QALY Procedure', *Social Science and Medicine*, **29**, 469–77.

Charny, M.C., P.A. Lewis and S.C. Farrow (1989), 'Choosing who shall not be treated in the NHS', *Social Science and Medicine*, **28**, 1331–8.

Cohen, G.A. (1993), 'Equality of What? On Welfare, Goods and Capabilities,' in Martha C. Nussbaum and Amartya Sen (eds), *The Quality of Life*, Oxford: Clarendon Press.

Cohen, Joshua (1996), 'Preferences, needs and QALYs', *Journal of Medical Ethics*, **22** (5), 267–72.

Cook, J., J. Richardson and A. Street (1994), 'A cost utility analysis of treatment options for gallstone disease: methodological issues and results', *Health Economics*, **3**, 157–68.

Cooper, B. and W. Brodie (1976), '1972 life time earnings by age, sex, race and education level', Research and Statistics Note no. 12, Washington, US Department of Health, Education and Welfare.

Crosthwaite, Jan (1995), 'Moral Expertise: A Problem in the Professional Ethics of Professional Ethicists', *Bioethics*, **9** (5), 361–79.

Culyer, A.J. and A. Wagstaff (1992), 'QALYs versus HYEs: A Theoretical Exposition', Centre for Health Economics, discussion paper no. 99, University of York.

Culyer, A.J. and A. Wagstaff (1995), 'QALYs versus HYEs: A Reply to Gafni, Birch and Mehrez', *Journal of Health Economics*, **14** (1), 39–47.

Daniels, Norman (1979a), 'Wide Reflective Equilibrium and Theory Acceptance in Ethics', *The Journal of Philosophy*, **76**, 256–82.

Daniels, Norman (1979b), 'Rights to Health Care and Distributive Justice: Programmatic Worries', *The Journal of Medicine and Philosophy*, **4** (2), 174–91.

Daniels, Norman (1981), 'Health–Care Needs and Distributive Justice', *Philosophy and Public Affairs*, **10** (2), 146–79.

Daniels, Norman (1982), 'Equity of Access to Health Care: Some Conceptual and Ethical Issues', *Milbank Memorial Fund Quarterly*, **60** (1), 51–81.

Daniels, Norman (1983), 'Justice between Age Groups: Am I My Parents' Keeper?', *Milbank Memorial Fund Quarterly*, **61** (3), 489–522.

Daniels, Norman (1988), *Am I My Parents' Keeper?: An Essay on Justice Between The Young And The Old*, New York: Oxford University Press.

Daniels, Norman (1989), 'The Biomedical Model and Just Health Care: Reply to Jecker', *The Journal of Medicine and Philosophy*, **14** (6), 677–80.

Daniels, Norman (1993), 'Rationing Fairly: Programmatic Considerations', *Bioethics*, **7** (2/3), 224–33.

Diamond, D. and J. Hausman (1994), 'Contingent valuation: Is some number better than no number?', *Journal of Economic Perspectives*, **8**, 45–64.

Dolan, P., C. Gudex, P. Kind and A. Williams (1996a), 'The time trade-off method: results from a general population study', *Health Economics*, **5**, 141–54.

Dolan, P., C. Gudex, P. Kind and A. Williams (1996b), 'Valuing health states: A comparison of methods', *Journal of Health Economics*, **15**, 209–31.

Dostoevsky, F. (1994), *The Karamazov Brothers*, trans. Ignat Avsey, Oxford: Oxford University Press; first published 1879.

Dworkin, Ronald (1977), *Taking Rights Seriously*, London: Duckworth.

Elster, Jon (1991), 'Local Justice and Interpersonal Comparisons', in Jon Elster and John E. Roemer (eds), *Interpersonal Comparisons of Well-Being*, Cambridge: Cambridge University Press.

EuroQoL Group (1990), 'EuroQoL – a new facility for the measurement of health-related quality of life', *Health Policy*, **16**, 199–208.

Feeny, D., G. Torrance and W. Furlong (1996), 'Health utilities index', in B. Spilker (ed.), *Quality of Life and Pharmacoeconomics in Clinical Trials*, Philadelphia: Lippincott-Raven Publishers.

Freeman, Samuel (1994), 'Utilitarianism, Deontology, and the Priority of Right', *Philosophy and Public Affairs*, **23** (4), 313–49.

Fried, Charles (1976), 'Equality and Rights in Medical Care', *The Hastings Center Report*, **6** (1), 29–34.

Froberg, Debra G. and Robert L. Kane (1989), 'Methodology for Measuring Health-State Preferences', *Journal of Clinical Epidemiology*, **42**, 345–54, 459–71, 585–92, 675–85.

Frohlich, Norman and Joe A. Oppenheimer (1992), *Choosing Justice: An Experimental Approach to Ethical Theory*, Berkeley: University of California Press.

Glover, Jonathan (1977), *Causing Death and Saving Lives*, Harmondsworth: Penguin Books.

Gudex, C. (1994), 'EuroQoL state valuations from the general population: The visual analogue method', Health Economists Study Group, Newcastle, 6–8 July.

Hanemann, W. (1994), 'Valuing environment through contingent valuation', *Journal of Economic Perspectives*, **8**, 19–43.

Hare, R.M. (1963), *Freedom and Reason*, Oxford: Oxford University Press.

Hare, R.M. (1975), 'Rawls' Theory of Justice', in Norman Daniels (ed.), *Reading Rawls: Critical Studies on Rawls' 'A Theory of Justice'*, Stanford: Stanford University Press.

Hare, R.M. (1981), *Moral Thinking*, Oxford: Oxford University Press.

Hare, R.M. (1993a), 'Could Kant Have been a Utilitarian?', *Utilitas*, **5** (1), 1–16.

Hare, R.M. (1993b), 'Is medical ethics lost?', *Journal of Medical Ethics*, **19** (2), 69–70.

Harris, John (1985), *The Value of Life*, London: Routledge & Kegan Paul.

Harris, John (1987), 'QALYfying the value of life', *Journal of Medical Ethics*, **13** (3), 117–123.

Harris, John (1988), 'More and Better Justice', in J.M. Bell and Susan Mendus (eds), *Philosophy and Medical Welfare*, Cambridge: Cambridge University Press.

Harris, John (1994), 'Does Justice Require That We Be Ageist?', *Bioethics*, **8** (1), 74–83.

Harris, John (1995), 'Double jeopardy and the veil of ignorance – A reply', *Journal of Medical Ethics*, **21** (3), 151–7.

Harris, John (1996), 'Would Aristotle have played Russian Roulette?', *Journal of Medical Ethics*, **22** (4), 209–15.

Haveman, Robert H. (1970), 'Evaluating Public Expenditures Under Conditions of Unemployment', in Robert H. Haveman and Julius Margolis (eds), *Public Expenditures and Policy Analysis*, Chicago: Markham Publishing Co.

Hawthorne, G. and J. Richardson (1996), 'An Australian MAU/QALY instrument: Rationale and preliminary results', Centre for Health Program Evaluation, working paper no. 49, Monash University, Melbourne.

Hope, T., D. Sprigings and R. Crisp (1993), '"Not Clinically Indicated": Patients' Interests or Resource Allocation?', *British Medical Journal*, **306**, 379–381.

Jamieson, Dale (1988), 'Is Applied Ethics Worth Doing?', in David M. Rosenthal and Fadlou Shehadi (eds), *Applied Ethics and Ethical Theory*, Salt Lake City: University of Utah Press.

Jecker, Nancy S. (1989), 'Towards a Theory of Age-Group Justice', *The Journal of Medicine and Philosophy*, **14** (6), 655–76.

Johannesson, M. (1995), 'Quality adjusted life years versus health year equivalence – A comment', *Journal of Health Economics*, **14** (1), 9–17.

Kahneman, Daniel and Carol Varey (1991), 'Notes on the Psychology of Utility', in Jon Elster and John E. Roemer (eds), *Interpersonal Comparisons of Well-Being*, Cambridge: Cambridge University Press.

Kant, Immanuel (1948), *The Groundwork of the Metaphysic of Morals*, trans. H.J. Paton, London: Hutchinson; first published 1785.

Kaplan, R., J. Bush and C. Berry (1976), 'Health status: Types of validity and the index of well being', *Health Services Research*, **11** (4), 478–507.

Kaplan, R. and J. Bush (1982), 'Health-related quality of life measurement for evaluation research and policy analysis', *Health Psychology*, **1**, 61–80.

Kaplan, R., J. Anderson and T. Ganiats (1993), 'The Quality of Well-being Scale: Rationale for a single quality of life index', in Stewart R. Walker and Rachel M. Rosser (eds), *Quality of Life Assessment: Key Issues in the 1990s*, Dordrecht: Kluwer Academic Publishers.

Kappel, Klemens and Peter Sandøe (1992), 'QALYs, Age and Fairness', *Bioethics*, **6** (4), 297–316.

Kazan, P. (1990), 'The diplomacy of consultation: Policies and strategies for community consultation', *Proceedings of the National Ethnic Health Policy Conference*, Adelaide: South Australian Health Commission.

Kind, P. and R. Rosser (1988), 'The qualification of health', *European Journal of Social Psychology*, **18**, 63–77.

Klarman, Herbert E. (1965), 'Syphilis Control Programs', in R. Dorfman (ed.), *Measuring Benefits of Government Investments*, Washington, DC: Brookings Institution.

Klarman, Herbert E. (1982), 'The Road to Cost–Effectiveness Analysis', *Milbank Memorial Fund Quarterly*, **60** (4), 585–603.

Kuhse, Helga and Peter Singer (1988), 'Age and the Allocation of Medical Resources', *The Journal of Medicine and Philosophy*, **13** (1), 101–16.

Kymlicka, Will (1990), *Contemporary Political Philosophy*, Oxford: Clarendon Press.

Lewis, P.A. and M. Charny (1989), 'Which of two individuals do you treat when only their ages are different and you can't treat both?', *Journal of Medical Ethics*, **15** (1), 28–32.

Lockwood, Michael (1988), 'Quality of Life and Resource Allocation', in J.M. Bell and Susan Mendus (eds), *Philosophy and Medical Welfare*, Cambridge: Cambridge University Press.

Loomes, Graham (1995), 'The Myth of the HYE', *Journal of Health Economics*, **14** (1), 1–9.

Loomes, Graham and Lynda McKenzie (1989), 'The use of QALYs in health care decision making', *Social Science and Medicine*, **28** 299–308.

Martin, R. (1985), *Rawls and Rights*, Lawrence, Kansas: University Press of Kansas.

Maynard, A. (1987), 'Logic in Medicine: An Economic Perspective', *British Medical Journal*, **295**, 1537–41.

Maynard, A. (1991), 'Developing the health care market', *Economic Journal*, **101**, 1277–86.

McDermott, L. (1990), 'Speaking for Myself: The Challenge of Consultation in Multicultural Australia', *Migrant News*, November.

McKerlie, Dennis (1988), 'Egalitarianism and the Separateness of Persons', *Canadian Journal of Philosophy*, **18** (2), 205–25.

McKerlie, Dennis (1996), 'Equality', *Ethics*, **106** (2), 274–96.

McTurk, Lesley (1994), 'Using QALYs to allocate resources: A critique of some objections', *Monash Bioethics Review*, **13** (1), 22–31.

Mehrez, Abraham and Amiram Gafni (1989), 'Quality-adjusted life years, utility theory and healthy-years equivalents', *Medical Decision Making*, **9** (2), 142–9.

Menzel, Paul T. (1983), *Medical Costs, Moral Choices: A Philosophy of Health Care Economics in America*, New Haven: Yale University Press.

Messick, D.M. and K. Sentis (1983), 'Fairness, Preference, and Fairness Biases', in D.M. Messick and K. Cook (eds), *Equity Theory*, New York: Praeger.

Mill, John Stuart (1962), *Essays on Politics and Culture by J.S. Mill*, (ed.), *Gertrude Himmelfarb*, New York: Doubleday.

Mill, John Stuart (1973), *Utilitarianism* and *On Liberty*, New York: Anchor Press/Doubleday.

Misham, E.J. (1971), 'Evaluation of Life and Limb', *Journal of Political Economy*, **79** (4), 687–705.

Mooney, Gavin (1989), 'QALYs: Are they enough? A health economist's perspective', *Journal of Medical Ethics*, **15** (3), 148–52.

Mooney, Gavin and Jan Abel Olsen (1994), 'QALYs: Where Next?', in Alistair McGuire, Paul Fenn and Ken Mayhew (eds), *Providing Health Care: The Economics of Finance and Delivery*, Oxford: Oxford University Press.

Murry, C. and A. Lopez (1996), *The Global Burden of Disease*, published by the Harvard School of Public Health on behalf of the WHO and the World Bank, Harvard: Harvard University Press.

Mushkin, Selma J. (1962), 'Health As An Investment', *Journal of Political Economy*, **70** (5), 129–57.

Mushkin, Selma J. and J. Steven Landefeld (1979), *Biomedical Research: Costs and Benefits*, Cambridge, Mass.: Ballinger Publishing Co.

Nagel, Thomas (1975), 'Rawls on Justice', in Norman Daniels (ed.), *Reading Rawls: Critical Studies on Rawls' 'A Theory of Justice'*, Oxford: Basil Blackwell.

Najman, Jackob and Sol Levine (1981), 'Evaluating the Impact of Medical Care and Technologies on the Quality of Life: A Review and Critique', *Social Science and Medicine*, **15**, 107–15.

Nickel, James W. (1988), 'Philosophy and Policy', in David M. Rosenthal and Fadlou Shehadi (eds), *Applied Ethics and Ethical Theory*, Salt Lake City: University of Utah Press.

Nielsen, Kai (1997), 'Radical Welfare Egalitarianism', in Louis P. Pojman and Robert Westmoreland (eds), *Equality: Selected Readings*, Oxford: Oxford University Press.

Nietzsche, Friedrich (1955), *Beyond Good and Evil*, trans. Marianne Cowan, Chicago: Henry Regnery Company; first published 1886.

NOAA (National Oceanic and Atmospheric Administration) (1993), 'Report of the NOAA Panel on Contingent Valuation', *Federal Register*, **58**, 4601–14.

Nord, Erik (1990), 'A comment on the meaning of numerical valuations of health states', *Social Science and Medicine*, **30**, 943–4.

Nord, Erik (1991), 'Methods for Establishing Quality Weights for Life Years', National Centre for Health Program Evaluation, working paper no. 8, Monash University, Melbourne.

Nord, Erik (1993a), 'The relevance of health state after treatment in prioritising between different patients', *Journal of Medical Ethics,* **19** (1), 37–42.

Nord, Erik (1993b), 'Norwegian health care politicians are not concerned about maximizing health gains per crown', *Journal of the Norwegian Medical Association,* **113**, 1371–3 (text in Norwegian).

Nord, Erik (1996), 'Health state index models for use in resource allocation decisions', *International Journal of Technology Assessment in Health Care,* **12** (1), 31–44.

Nord, E., J. Richardson and K. Macarounas-Kirchmann (1993), 'Social evaluation of health care versus personal evaluation of health states', *International Journal of Technology Assessment in Health Care,* **9** (4), 463–78.

Nord, E., A. Street, H. Kuhse and P. Singer (1996), 'The significance of age and duration of effect in social evaluation of health care', *Health Care Analysis,* **4**, 103–11.

Nord, E., J. Richardson, A. Street, H. Kuhse and P. Singer (1995a), 'Maximising Health Benefits vs Egalitarianism: An Australian Survey of Health Issues', *Social Science and Medicine,* **41**, 1429–37.

Nord, E., J. Richardson, A. Street, H. Kuhse and P. Singer (1995b), 'Who cares about cost? Does economic analysis impose or reflect social values?', *Health Policy,* **34**, 79–94.

Norwegian Commission on Prioritising in Health Care (1987), *NOU,* 23, Oslo: Universitetsforlaget.

Note, D. (1969), 'Scarce Medical Resources', *Columbia Law Review,* **69**, 620–92.

Olsen, Jan Abel (1993), 'On What Basis Should Health Be Discounted?', *Journal of Health Economics,* **12**, 39–53.

Olsen, Jan Abel (1994), 'Persons vs years: two ways of eliciting implicit weights', *Health Economics,* **3** (1), 39–46.

Parfit, Derek (1973), 'Later Selves and Moral Principles', in Alan Montefiore (ed.), *Philosophy and Personal Relations: An Anglo-French Study,* London: Routledge & Kegan Paul.

Parfit, Derek (1984), *Reasons and Persons,* Oxford: Clarendon Press.

Parsonage, Michael and Henry Neuburger (1992), 'Discounting and Health Benefits', *Health Economics,* **1** (1), 71–6.

Pearlman, Robert A. and Richard F. Uhlmann (1988), 'Quality of Life in Chronic Diseases: Perceptions of Elderly Patients', *Journal of Gerontology,* **43** (2), M25–30.

Pogge, T. (1989), *Realizing Rawls,* Ithaca: Cornell University Press.

Pojman, Louis P. and Robert Westmoreland (eds) (1997), *Equality: Selected Readings,* Oxford: Oxford University Press.

Pool, Ithiel de Sola (1980), 'The New Censorship of Social Research', *The Public Interest,* Spring, 57–66.

Rakowski, Eric (1997), 'A Critique of Welfare Egalitarianism', in Louis

P. Pojman and Robert Westmoreland (eds), *Equality: Selected Readings*, Oxford: Oxford University Press.

Rawles, John (1989), 'Castigating QALYs', *Journal of Medical Ethics*, **15** (3), 143–7.

Rawles, John and Kate Rawles (1990), 'The QALY argument: A physician's and a philosopher's view', *Journal of Medical Ethics*, **16** (2), 93–4.

Rawls, John (1971), *A Theory of Justice*, London: Oxford University Press.

Rawls, John (1982), 'Social unity and the primary goods', in A.K. Sen and B. Williams (eds), *Utilitarianism and Beyond*, Cambridge: Cambridge University Press.

Rawls, John (1988), 'The Priority of Right and Ideas of the Good', *Philosophy and Public Affairs*, **17** (4), 251–76.

Rescher, Nicholas (1966), *Distributive Justice: A Constructive Critique of the Utilitarian Theory of Distribution*, Indianapolis/New York/Kansas City: Bobbs–Merrill.

Rice, Dorothy P. and Barbara S. Cooper (1967), 'The Economic Value of Human Life', *American Journal of Public Health*, **57** (11), 1954–66.

Richardson, Jeffrey (1987), 'The accountant as triage master: An economist's perspective on voluntary euthanasia', *Bioethics*, **1** (3), 226–41.

Richardson, Jeffrey (1991), 'Economic assessment of health care: Theory and practice', *Australian Economic Review*, first quarter, 1–21.

Richardson, Jeffrey (1994), 'Cost–Utility Analyses: What Should Be Measured?', *Social Science and Medicine*, **39**, 7–21.

Richardson, Jeffrey and Johanna Cook (1992), 'The QALY: Victim of Misinformation', National Centre for Health Program Evaluation, Monash University, Melbourne.

Richardson, J. and E. Nord (1997), 'The importance of perspective in the measurement of quality adjusted life years', *Medical Decision Making*, **17** (1), 33–41.

Richardson, J., J. Hall and G. Salkeld (1989), 'Cost–Utility Analysis: The Compatibility of Measurement Techniques and the Measurement of Utility Through Time', in *Economics and Health: 1989*, Proceedings of the Eleventh Australian Conference of Health Economists, C. Selby Smith (ed.), Public Sector Management Institute, Monash University, Melbourne.

Richardson, J., J. Hall and G. Salkeld (1996), 'The measurement of utility in multi-phase health states', *International Journal of Technology Assessment in Health Care*, **12** (1), 151–62.

Robinson, James C. (1986), 'Philosophic origins of the economic valuation of life', *Milbank Memorial Fund Quarterly*, **64** (1), 133–55.

Robinson, James C. (1990), 'Philosophical Origins of the Social Rate of Discount in Cost–Benefit Analysis', *Milbank Memorial Fund Quarterly*, **68** (2), 245–65.

Ross, W.D. (1930), *The Right and the Good*, Oxford: Clarendon Press.

Rosser, R. (1993), 'A health index and output measure', in Stuart R. Walker and Rachel M. Rosser (eds), *Quality of Life Assessment: Key Issues in the 1990s*, Dordrecht: Kluwer Academic Publishers.

Rosser, R. and P. Kind (1978), 'A Scale of Evaluations of States of Illness: Is There a Social Consensus?', *International Journal of Epidemiology*, **7**, 347–58.

Russell, L. (1992), 'Opportunity costs in modern medicine', *Health Affairs*, Summer, 162–9.

Sackett, D.L. and G.W. Torrance (1978), 'The Utility of Different Health States as Perceived by the General Public', *Journal of Chronic Diseases*, **7**, 347–58.

Scanlon, T.M. (1975), 'Rawls' Theory of Justice', in Norman Daniels (ed.), *Reading Rawls*, Oxford: Basil Blackwell.

Schoemaker, P. (1982), 'The expected utility model: Its variance, purposes, evidence and limitations', *Journal of Economic Literature*, **20** (2), 529–63.

Sen, A.K. (1989), 'Rawls versus Bentham: An Axiomatic Examination of the Pure Distribution Problem', in Norman Daniels (ed.), *Reading Rawls: Critical Studies on Rawls' 'A Theory of Justice'*, Stanford: Stanford University Press.

Sintonen, H. (1981), 'An approach to measuring and valuing health states', *Social Science and Medicine*, **15**, 55–65.

Sintonen, H. (1994), 'The 15D measure of health-related quality of life: Reliability, validity and sensitivity of its health state descriptive system', working paper no. 41, National Centre for Health Program Evaluation, Monash University, Melbourne.

Sintonen, H. (1995), 'The 15D measure of health-related quality of life: Feasibility, reliability and validity of its valuation system', working paper no. 42, National Centre for Health Program Evaluation, Monash University, Melbourne.

Sintonen, H. and M. Pekurinen (1993), 'A fifteen-dimensional measure of health-related quality of life (15D) and its applications', in Stuart R. Walker and Rachel M. Rosser (eds), *Quality of Life Assessment: Key Issues in the 1990s*, Dordrecht: Kluwer Academic Publishers.

Smart, J.J.C. (1987), *Essays Metaphysical and Moral*, Oxford: Basil Blackwell.

Smart, J.J.C. and Bernard Williams (1973), *Utilitarianism: For and Against*, Cambridge: Cambridge University Press.

Smith, Alwyn (1987), 'Qualms About QALYs', *The Lancet*, **1**, 1134–6.

Smith, R. (1996), 'Is regret theory an alternative basis for estimating the value of health care interventions?', *Health Policy*, **37**, 105–15.

Temkin, Larry S. (1993), *Inequality*, New York: Oxford University Press.

Torrance, George W. (1986), 'Measurement of Health State Utilities for Economic Appraisal: A Review', *Journal of Health Economics*, **5** (1), 1–30.

Torrance, George W. (1987), 'Utility approach to measuring health related quality of life', *Journal of Chronic Diseases*, **40** (6), 593–600.

Torrance, G., W. Furlong, D. Feeney and M. Boyle (1995), 'Multi-attribute preference functions: Health utilities index', *Pharmacoeconomics*, **7** (6), 503–20.

Torrance, G., Y. Zhang, D. Feeney, W. Furlong and R. Barr (1992), 'Multi-attribute preference functions for a comprehensive health status classification system', Centre for Health Economics and Policy Analysis, Working paper no. 92–8, McMaster University, Hamilton, Ontario.

Van Agt, H., M. Essink-Bot, P. Krabbe and G. Bonsel (1994), 'Test–retest reliability of health state valuations collected with the EuroQoL questionnaire', *Social Science and Medicine*, **39** (11), 1537–44.

Viscousi, K. (1993), 'The value of risks to life and health', *Journal of Economic Literature*, **31**, 1912–46.

Vlastos, Gregory (1962), 'Justice and Equality', in Richard B. Brandt (ed.), *Social Justice*, Englewood Cliffs, NJ: Prentice-Hall.

Wagstaff, Adam (1991), 'QALYs and the Equity–efficiency Trade-off', *Journal of Health Economics*, **10** (1), 21–41.

Warner, K. and B. Luce (1982), *Cost Benefit and Cost Effectiveness Analysis in Health Care: Principles, Practice and Potential*, Ann Arbor, Mich.: Health Administration Press.

Weinstein, Milton C. (1984), 'Cost–Effectiveness of Technologies for Heart Disease,' in Paul Gross and Colleen McMahon (eds), *New Technologies for the Reduction of Health Costs: International Policy Perspectives for the 80s and Beyond*, Sydney: Institute of Health Economics and Technology Assessment.

Weisbrod, B.A. (1971), 'Costs and Benefits of Medical Research: A Case Study of Poliomyelitis', *Journal of Political Economy*, **79**, 527–44.

Williams, Alan, (1981), 'Welfare economics and health status measurement', in Jacques van der Graag and Mark Perlman (eds), *Health, Economics and Health Economics*, Elsevier: North-Holland.

Williams, Alan (1985), 'Economics of Coronary Artery Bypass Grafting', *British Medical Journal*, **291**, 326–9.

Williams, Alan (1988), 'Ethics and Efficiency in the Provision of Health Care', in J.M. Bell and Susan Mendus (eds), *Philosophy and Medical Welfare*, Cambridge: Cambridge University Press.

Williams, Alan (1997), 'Intergenerational Equity: An Exploration of the Fair Innings Argument', *Health Economics*, **6** (2), 117–32.

Williams, Bernard (1972), *Morality: An Introduction to Ethics*, London: Cambridge University Press.

Wright, S.J. (1986), 'Age, sex and health: a summary of findings from the York Health Evaluation Survey', discussion paper no. 15, Centre for Health Economics, University of York.

Index

access, equality of 49
act-utilitarianism 11
adaptation 27
Aday, L.A. 83
age discrimination
    fair innings argument 48–51, 60–1
    prudential lifespan approach 55–9
    QALYs 47–8, 51, 53–5
    slippery slope problem 59–60
    social hijacking 63–4
age-relative opportunity range 56
ageism *see* age discrimination
Andersen, R. 83
Aristotle 107
Australia, QALY maximization
    survey 118–26, *121*
autonomy 67, 86

Baron, Jonathan 63
Battin, Margaret P. 53
Beauchamp, Tom L. 91
benefits 15
    economic analysis *18*
    maximization 124
    needs 85–6
    objection to balancing view 88–9
    QALYs 38–9, 42
Bentham, Jeremy 10
big differences problem 102
Bowling, A. 24
Brooks, Richard G. 24
budgets, value of life 2–4

Campbell, Alastair V. 78–9
cancer 30–31
Carr-Hill, Roy A. 36
categorical imperative 9, 61
CBA *see* cost-benefit analysis

CEA *see* cost-effectiveness analysis
Childress, James F. 91
choice
    individual 3
    rational 55, 109–15
cigarette smoking 125–6
Cohen, G.A. 63
Cohen, Joshua 111
community values 4, 117, 126
compensation objection 78, 79–81
complaints 87–8
consequentialism 9, 10
contingent valuation 37
Cooper, Barbara S. 17
cost minimization *18*
cost-benefit analysis (CBA) 15–17,
    18
cost-effectiveness analysis (CEA)
    18, 21
cost-per-QALY prioritizing rule 47–
    8, 52–4, 59
cost-utility analysis (CUA) 16, *18*, 22
costs 15
Crisp, R. 47, 84
CUA *see* cost-utility analysis
cultural relativism 7

DALY *see* Disability Adjusted Life
    Year
Daniels, Norman 49, 55–8, 62
death
    postponement 65–6
    risk of 20
decisions, informed 129–30
Diamond, D. 38
difference principle 84, 107–8
Disability Adjusted Life Year
    (DALY) 26

discrimination
  see also age discrimination
  community values 118–26
  threshold of 66–7
  unjust 106
disease-specific measurement
    instruments 24
distributive neutrality 117–18, 120,
    122–6
  difficulty of choice *121*
Dostoevsky, F. 9
double jeopardy 99–101
duties 12
Dworkin, Ronald 106

economic evaluation 15–22, *18*
effectiveness, unit of 21
effects, valuation of 16
efficiency, need reconciliation 89–91
egalitarianism 126
  QALYs 40–1, 47, 54
emotivism 6
equal distribution 5
equality of access 49
equity
  see also fairness; justice
  need objection 83
equity objection 77, 81–3
ethical neutrality 127
ethics
  Kantian 61–2
  normative 5, 9, 12
  QALYs 38–43
expectations 36
expert committees 128–31, 133
externalities 17
extravagants 63

fair innings argument 48–51, 60–1,
    79
fairness 15
  see also equity; justice
  QALYs 60–61, 75, 77
family responsibilities 125
Fleming, G.V. 83
free market allocation 4
Freeman, Samuel 90
Froberg, Debra G. 33
Frolich, Norman 91

Gafni, Amiram 30
gallstone surgery 31
generic instruments 24
Gillett, Grant 78–9
Glover, Jonathan 64
good, nature of 3
greed 63

Hare, R.M. 7, 12, 92
Harris, John
  age discrimination 47, 48, 64–7
  double jeopardy 99–104, 106–15
Hausman, J. 38
health improvement, comparison 24
health professionals, QALYs 34–5
health states assessment
  general public 35–6
  health professionals 34–5
  instruments 25–7
  patients 33–4
  preferences 26–7
  QALYs 30–31
  quality of life 24
  utilities *29*
Health Utility Index (HUI) 26
Healthy Year Equivalent (HYE) 30
Hope, T. 47, 84
HUI *see* Health Utility Index
human capital approach 17, 19
HYE *see* Healthy Year Equivalent

illness, moral arbitrariness 84–5
impartiality 86
income distribution 4, 91
individuals
  choice 3
  discrimination 64–8
  equal value of life 103–4
infertility 56
influenza vaccination 21
informed decisions 129–30
instruments 24–7
insurance 4
intuitionism 9

Jecker, Nancy S. 57
justice 5
  see also equity; fairness
  as fairness 83

safety net objection 92

Kane, Robert L. 33
Kant, Immanuel 9–10
Kantian ethics 61–2
Kappel, Klemens 49, 79–80
Kuhse, H. 119
Kymlicka, Will 83, 91

life
    enjoyment of 63, 85–6
    equal value of 103–4
    interest in 110
    market value 19
    value of 1–4, 20
life expectancy 51, 65–7
life saving treatments 53, 120, 122
life-time view 79
lifestyle 118
Locke, John 13
Lockwood, Michael 41, 49–50, 83
Loomes, Graham 35–6, 41

McKenzie, Lynda 35–6, 41
McKerlie, Dennis 82–3
McTurk, Lesley 40
magnitude estimation 27
market failures 17
Martin, R. 83
Marx, Karl 5, 6
material welfare 17, 39
MAU *see* multi-attribute utility
maximin strategy 14, 108
Mehrez, Abraham 30
meta-ethical analysis 5–8
Mill, John Stuart 11, 13, 90
Misham, E.J. 20
Mooney, Gavin 36
moral theories 130
morality
    arbitrariness of illness 84–5
    inescapability of 5
multi-attribute utility (MAU)
        instruments 25–6
Mushkin, Selma J. 17

Nagel, Thomas 87
natural lottery 93
need, efficiency reconciliation 89–91

need objection 77, 83–91
Nietzsche, Friedrich 5
Nord, Erik 28, 119
normal species functioning 55–8
normative ethics 5, 9, 12
Nottingham Health Profile 24

objection to balancing view 88–9
Olsen, Jan Abel 36, 117–18
Oppenheimer, Joe A. 91
opportunity costs 15
Oregon Experiment 26
organ transplantation 123–4

paraplegia 73–5
Parfit, Derek 88–9
paternalism 3, 4
patients, QALYs assessment 33–4
person trade-off (PTO) 28–9, 32
Plato 5
pneumonia vaccination 21
Pogge, T. 83
preference utilitarianism 10–11
    QALYs 39–41
present time view 79
prima facie duties 12
priority 118
probable gain 109
prudential lifespan approach 55–9
PTO *see* person trade-off
public opinion 127–8

QALY *see* quality-adjusted life year
QoL *see* quality of life index factor
quality of life 65, 122
quality of life index factor (QoL) 22,
    24
    calculations 73–4, **74, 76, 77**
Quality of Well Being (QWB) 26, 27
quality-adjusted life year (QALY)
    age discrimination 47–8, 51, 53–5
    calculations 99–100
    competing therapies *23*
    cost-utility analysis *18*, 22
    distributive neutrality 117–18
    eligibility for survival 111–14
    ethical neutrality 127
    ethics 38–43
    fair innings argument 48–51

fairness 60–1
gains 74–6
Healthy Year Equivalent 30
maximization 52–5, 64–8, 74–5
maximization survey 118–26, *121*
measurement 24–9
measurement problems 32
need/efficiency reconciliation 89–91
prudential lifespan approach comparison 58–9
sensitivity 102
slippery slope problem 59–60
social hijacking 62–4
stated and revealed preferences 37–8
utilitarianism 61–2, 67, 78–9, 84, 90
veil of ignorance 105–6, 111
QWB *see* Quality of Well Being

random allocation 101–3
eligibility for survival 111–14
rational choice 55, 109–15
rational egoism 105, 109–10
Rawles, John 47, 83–4
Rawls, John
difference principle 107–8
justice 13, 83–4
reflective equilibrium 8–9
social hijacking 62
veil of ignorance 105
reason 129
reconciliationist view 89–90
reflective equilibrium 8–9
regret theory 31
Rescher, Nicholas 93
Rice, Dorothy P. 17
Richardson, J. 119
rights 13
risk, value of 20
road safety 1
Ross, W.D. 12
rule-utilitarianism 11–12

sacrifices 88
safety net objection 78, 91–4
Sandøe, Peter 49, 79–80
saturation 27
scaling techniques 25–7

Scanlon, T.M. 87
scenario approach 27
self-interest 31
self-serving biases 35
Sen, A.K. 89–90, 93
sensitivity 102
SF36 24
SG *see* standard gamble
Sickness Impact Profile 24
slavery 106–7
slippery slope problem, QALYs 59–60
Smart, J.J.C. 86–7
Smith, Alwyn 47
Smith, R. 31
smoking 125–6
social contract ethics 13
social hijacking, QALYs 62–4
social values 20
Sola Pool, I. de 131
spending limits 3
Springings, D. 47, 84
standard gamble (SG) 28
state paternalism 4
stated preference technique 37–8
Street, A. 119
subjectivism 6–7
suffering, compensation 80–1
survival, eligibility for 111–14

Temkin, Larry S. 87–8
Ten Commandments 9
threshold of discrimination 66–7
time trade-off (TTO) 28, *29*
Torrance, George W. 35
TTO *see* time trade-off

universal prescriptivism 7
unjust discrimination 106
utilitarianism 10, 41
see also act-utilitarianism; preference utilitarianism; rule-utilitarianism
age discrimination 54–5, 61–2
difference principle 84
quality of life 78–9
rational choice 90
threshold discrimination 67
utilities, health states *29*

utility 5
  gain 109
  maximization 52–5, 67
utility index 22–3

vaccinations 21
value
  costs 15
  criterion 19
veil of ignorance 13, 104–8

identity concealed 114
Viscousi, K. 20
von Neumann-Morgenstern axioms
  28

welfarism, QALYs 39
Williams, Alan 84, 118
Williams, Bernard 86–7
willingness to pay approach 19
Wright, S.J. 118